Fisher

THE MOUNTAINEERS, founded in 1906, is a non-profit outdoor activity and conservation club, whose mission is "to explore, study, preserve and enjoy the natural beauty of the outdoors . . ." Based in Seattle, Washington, the club is now the third largest such organization in the United States, with 12,000 members and four branches throughout Washington State.

The Mountaineers sponsors both classes and year-round outdoor activities in the Pacific Northwest, which include hiking, mountain climbing, ski-touring, snowshoeing, bicycling, camping, kayaking and canoeing, nature study, sailing, and adventure travel. The club's conservation division supports environmental causes through educational activities, sponsoring legislation, and presenting informational programs. All club activities are led by skilled, experienced volunteers, who are dedicated to promoting safe and responsible enjoyment and preservation of the outdoors.

The Mountaineers Books, an active, non-profit publishing program of the club, produces guidebooks, instructional texts, historical works, natural history guides, and works on environmental conservation. All books produced by The Mountaineers are aimed at fulfilling the club's mission.

If you would like to participate in these organized outdoor activities or the club's programs, consider a membership in The Mountaineers. For information and an application, write or call The Mountaineers, Club Headquarters, 300 Third Avenue West, Seattle, Washington 98119; (206) 284-6310.

BOOKS BY THE MOUNTAINEERS

Other books you may enjoy from The Mountaineers:

Europe by Bike: 18 Tours Geared for Discovery, Whitehill. Detailed, point-to-point information on bicycling in England, Sweden, Denmark, Belgium, Holland, Germany, France, Austria, Italy, Yugoslavia, Greece, Spain, and Portugal.

Cycle Touring in New Zealand, Ringer. Guide to North and South Islands includes how-to and where-to information for 14 tours, plus trip planning, accomodations, and more.

Bicycle Touring in Australia, Hemmings. Detailed guidebook to 12 road-cycling tours covering the best, most popular, and most accessible areas for cyclists, plus road tips and trip planning.

Bicycling the Pacific Coast, 2nd Edition: A Complete Road Guide, Canada to Mexico, Kirkendall & V. Spring. Classic touring guide covers road conditions, availability of provisions, accessible campgrounds, and points of interest. Detailed daily mileage logs, elevation profiles, and maps.

The Best of Britain's Countryside: The Two-Week Traveler Series — A Walking & Driving Itinerary, North. Two-week, customized itineraries to the most romantic, rewarding places in Great Britain. Day-by-day route information includes directions, distance, region's cultural, and natural history, and "daily bread/daily bed" advice.

- Southern England.
- Northern England & Scotland.

The Pocket Doctor. 2nd Ed.: Your Ticket to Good Health While Traveling, Bezruchka, M.D. Completely updated and revised, covers jet lag, water, food, hygiene, health in different environments, treatments for common illnesses and bites, sprains, scrapes, infections, and other problems. Clear, concise instructions for life-threatening emergencies.

Bicycling Gearing, Marr. Complete gearing how-to and shifting strategies for all cyclists.

Available from your local book or outdoor store, or from The Mountaineers Books, 1011 SW Klickitat Way, Suite 107, Seattle, WA 98134. Or call for a catalog of over 200 outdoor books: 1-800-553-4453.

ENGLAND

BY BIKE
18 TOURS GEARED FOR DISCOVERY

ENGLAND
BY BIKE
18 TOURS GEARED FOR DISCOVERY

Les Woodland

THE MOUNTAINEERS

5 4 3 2
5 4 3 2 1

Published by The Mountaineers
1011 SW Klickitat Way, Seattle, Washington 98134

Published simultaneously in Canada by Douglas & McIntyre, Ltd., 1615 Venables Street, Vancouver, B.C. V5L 2H1

Published simultaneously in Great Britain by Cordee, 3a DeMontfort Street, Leicester, England, LE1 7HD

Manufactured in the United States of America

Edited by Kris Fulsaas
Maps by Carla Majernik
All photographs by the author unless otherwise noted.
Cover design by Elizabeth Watson
Book design by Bridget Culligan Design
Typography and Computer Layout by André Gene Samson of Word Graphics, Inc.

Cover photograph: Peace and freedom in Middle England; hours of quiet biking.
Frontispiece: They call it Bicycle Island; the rush for the Yarmouth Ferry explains why.

Library of Congress Cataloging in Publication Data
Woodland, Les.
    England by bike / Les Woodland
    p.   cm.
    Includes index.
    ISBN 0-89886-275-2
    1. Bicycle touring—Great Britain—Guidebooks. 2. Great Britain—Description
    and travel—1971-
GV1046.G7W66   1992
796.6'4'0941—dc20
                                                              92-16478
                                                                   CIP

CONTENTS

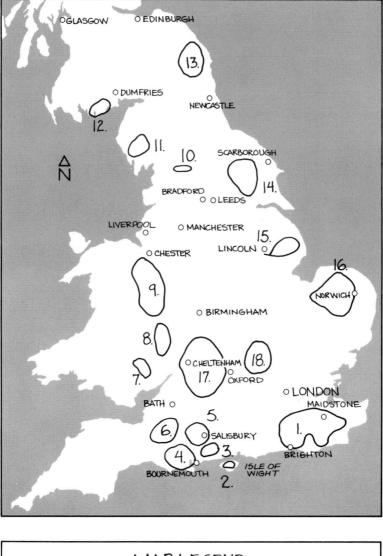

MAP LEGEND

A41→ "A" ROADS	.... FERRY
B3309→ "B" ROADS	→ DIRECTION OF TRAVEL
O CITY OR TOWN	─⌣ OFF-ROAD TRACK

PART I

INTRODUCTION

You can almost hear hooves ringing and see Victorian women in shawls and long dresses, can't you? This is Hockers Hill Street in Chepstow.

A CURIOUS COUNTRY

If ever a country were made for seeing by bicycle, it's England. Oh, it's crowded, sure enough. There are more cars to the mile than in any country in the world. And because they've got tighter suspensions and shorter dimensions than your average North American car, they're also driven faster and on narrower, more twisting roads.

But I stick to my claim. England is made for biking simply because there are millions of miles of country by-ways too small for through traffic to trouble with, and because the scenery and the accents and the attitude to life change literally every 50 miles.

If you haven't been before, I think that'll surprise you. You can tell from a person's voice his or her birthplace within about 30 miles, his or her education, and . . . this being England . . . his or her social class. John Steinbeck once said that however different you might think Texans, New Yorkers and Californian Chinese might be from each other, they all have much more in common than Welshmen with Englishmen, or the northern English from the Scottish, or the Highland and Lowland Scots. And I (born in London, living in East Anglia via the southeast) agree.

More than that, there are the kind of novelties that any other nation would have done away with years ago. Scotland, Northern Ireland, the Isle of Man, the Channel Islands and England and Wales all have their own currencies. Scottish money isn't legal tender in England (although it's generally accepted, since the English are as keen on money as anyone else), Channel Islands money won't be taken anywhere else, and the pound in Northern Ireland is worth more than the pound in southern Ireland.

Nor do the British worry particularly that the law in Scotland (which uses the Napoleonic code) is different from that in England and Wales and different again from Northern Ireland. The Isle of Man is a quite separate country which flogs ne'er-do-wells, fawns over millionaires, and hires Britain to protect it from invaders. The Channel Islands won't let you live there unless you're worth a fortune, and although Northern Ireland has its own government (albeit out of use during The Troubles), Scotland, Wales and, for that matter, England don't. As a matter of interest, it takes more government employees to administer Scotland than it takes to run the entire European Community.

So, given that the whole place is only about 700 miles top to bottom, don't you just itch to come and sort it out?

The idea of this book is to show you round my country, by bike, as you might show me round your hometown. Just as you wouldn't show me the junkyards next to the railroad, I'm not going to waste your time taking you from one prominent but dull national center to another. If you want to see Stratford-on-Avon or Trafalgar Square or the castle in Edinburgh, you don't need an insider to show you the way.

A fairy tale comes to life: Leeds Castle near Maidstone.

I also figure that some bits of Britain are too hilly for vacation cycling. We don't have mountains like some people have mountains (the highest classified road gets to 665 meters, between Braemar and Blairgowrie in Scotland), but they're still pretty high. What's more, because they haven't got much room to reach full height, they're mighty steep. More than that, British mountains are indecisive and go up and down several times before they finally have a proper go at it. That's why I say go to Devon and Cornwall by all means, but be aware that it's more walking than cycling country. In summer it's also full of men with shorts, sandals, patterned socks and thick glasses, towing trailers in wafts of gas fumes along lanes marginally narrower than their trailers.

The only exception I make to this rule is part of the Lake District in the English north-west, where the scenery more than compensates for a road so steep (more than one-in-three) that you feel seriously in danger of toppling over backward.

I don't suggest you cycle around London, not because it's dangerous (although I suppose it is, actually) but because it's tedious. You can

Alum Bay, Isle of Wight—charming but busy with visitors.

see all you want by walking or using public transport—and you won't have your bike stolen (see the Survival Skills section). I'll also tip you off about the places the tourist people harp on about—Stratford-upon-Avon ("come meet your fellow travelers")—and I warn you that Britain, if you haven't been here before, isn't all thatched cottages, quaint rustics in smocks, and spreading country lasses with peaches-and-cream complexions and shoulders made sturdy by toting milk churns. If you do see traditional maypole or country dancers (and you well might), you can bet your life that these days they're computer software salespeople to a person.

HOW TO USE THIS BOOK

Part I tells how to plan your trip, what to take, and survival skills. I'll explain the system—the rights of way, the signposting, the maps. I'll tell you how to escape the airports and how to organize your bed for the night. In Part II, I'll give you a selection of routes which, to me, typify Britain. I've chosen the routes to give you a slice of true Britain—or at least, that much of Britain that's (a) worth seeing and (b) doesn't have so few roads that a guide is unnecessary.

They run roughly clockwise round England, the Welsh borders and southern Scotland, with a great loop through middle England. I set out to write a series of one-day trips but I was defeated. So often, I'd get near someplace really interesting and be forced to turn back short or force you to ride 100 miles in a day. Instead, I settled for a mixture—circuits the most athletic could cover in one ride and bigger loops that make a multiday vacation of their own.

The general arrangement is that the routes start south of London, go south to the coast, then west along the sea edge, then north up along the edge of Wales and so on.

It's hard to guess how far you'll want to ride. The long loops are broken into sections, but that doesn't mean you're forced to ride a section each day. Accommodation isn't difficult to find on any of these routes, provided you don't leave it till too late in the day. And in the case of the first route, through southeastern England, I've drawn it so that you can pick sections and join or leave by train from London.

If you want a really long tour, several of the routes will join up to make something far longer. Where that's possible, I've given general directions for a scenic or quiet link. Where there's no link, it's because a connection would take you through depressing or built-up areas, such as the Manchester-Liverpool area, or across London. In other cases, the link won't be between adjacent chapters; I've kept the routes in approximate order, but sometimes a quirk of geography in this little island makes it possible to ride them out of order.

The links, by the way, don't come with the same recommendation (or for that matter the same detail) as the tours. They're just convenient ways of getting from one place to another, using minor rather than major roads wherever possible. It's important that you use them in conjunction with a good map. You will, of course, see interesting things along the way, but to list them all would make an impossibly long book.

PLANNING YOUR TRIP

PASSPORTS AND VISAS. You'll need a passport but not normally a visa, if you're a U.S. or Canadian citizen, but check before you come. Your passport will be stamped with a permit valid for three months, but it doesn't entitle you to work for money.

If you intend to stay longer, check with the British embassy before you leave. Note that the three months normally starts all over every time you leave the country (e.g., to visit France).

FINDING A BED AND MEALS. There is no shortage of accommodations in any of the areas covered in this book. It ranges from the grandest hotels down to so-called camping barns, which are little more than four walls and a roof.

The best way to meet the British is by staying bed-and-breakfast, or B-and-B. These are homes, sometimes farmhouses, with spare bedrooms. You have a room and use of a bath or shower, and you breakfast with the family. Often you'll be invited to spend the evening with the family—usually watching television—and some bed-and-breakfast places serve an evening meal as well if you book by lunchtime. Prices are about two-thirds of a moderate hotel, and standards are frequently higher. You'll spot B-and-B signs in villages and at farms.

Most towns have a hotel and bed-and-breakfast area, usually converted houses. Just ask. You can also buy guides to B-and-Bs at newsagents (usually chosen by category, such as farmhouses or vegetarian or whatever), and lists are always available at area tourist offices. (See the appendix for addresses.) You can book by phone. The larger tourist offices will book a bed for you, sometimes for several days ahead.

There's also a network of youth hostels affiliated to the Scottish and to the English and Welsh associations. To stay there, and to get a list, you have to belong to the youth hostel association at home. Membership is international. There are also a few independent hostels and camping barns, usually in mountainous areas, with primitive accommodations. You usually need to have a sleeping bag at least, sometimes more.

There is no problem about getting a meal on these routes. There are restaurants, or at least a café or fish-and-chip shop, in all but the tiniest communities. Takeaway food is popular—in addition to fish-and-chips, look for Chinese and Indian (actually usually Pakistani or Bangladeshi) food. The biggest main roads have restaurant chains such as Happy Eater and Little Chef every 10 miles or so. Most pubs serve lunch at attractive prices and sometimes an evening meal.

Pubs were once restricted to lunchtime and evening, from the days when munitions workers got drunk during the first world war and caused loud explosions. Now they open whenever they choose, except Sundays after about 2:30 P.M. This is better, except that now you never know just when, if at all, a pub will open during the day. Normally, you can expect it to open, at the least, from 12:30 P.M. to 2:30 P.M. and from 6:00 P.M. to 11:00 P.M.

Tipping is not expected, except in taxis, where 5 to 10 percent is appropriate. For restaurants, check whether a service charge has been added. By law, you don't have to pay it, although I've never known anybody to refuse.

Twenty-four-hour shopping is unknown. Most shops are open from 8:30 A.M. to 5:30 P.M. weekdays and Saturdays, although suburbs and minor towns still close early one afternoon a week (usually Tuesday, Wednesday or Thursday). A few small shops and supermarkets are open into the evening, but normally only in towns. It's possible to buy canned goods and other minor items at some gas stations.

Sunday opening is confused. The law is chaotic and increasingly broken. You can buy food on Sunday mornings without difficulty.

Small towns and some city centers have open-air markets weekly.

HEALTH. Britain has socialized medicine, paid from taxes and

Several youth hostels make the Solway Firth area attractive for protracted riding; this is Minnigaff, run to the movement's original simple guidelines.

given free or subsidized. While foreigners might get free immediate treatment for minor cuts, their insurance is expected to cover anything more.

MUD AND MAPS. Mud and maps go unavoidably together in Britain. The reason: all land in Britain belongs to someone and access to it varies according to the status of ancient paths. The status of that path should be shown wherever it leaves a surfaced road (that's what the law says, anyway), but the definitive guide is the Ordnance Survey map for the area.

The Ordnance Survey is a government institution which runs as a commercial operation. For the mandarins of Whitehall, the seat of British government, it provides accurate mapping of England, Scotland, Wales and the Isle of Man (not, you'll notice, any of the other islands, including Ireland and the Channel Islands). For other map companies, it provides the initial survey for their own productions. For local government (county and district councils), it records the rights of way that the council and history decree. And for people like you and me, it provides maps.

The Ordnance Survey is at Romsey Road, Southampton SO9 4DH, and its maps are available at most bookshops—the bigger the bookshop, the wider the selection. All mainland Britain and the immediate islands are covered by 204 sheets of 25 miles square at 2 cm to 1 km, which is about $1^1/_4$ in to 1 mile. This is the Landranger series, published in a lurid magenta cover with a photograph on the front. There are other maps and other scales, but this is the recognized map for off-road access.

MAIL. Post offices are open 9:00 A.M. to 5.30 P.M. weekdays and on Saturday mornings. Local shops sometimes also have a post office counter, although it'll keep its own hours.

There are two rates of post—first class, which tries to achieve next-day delivery, and second-class, which takes a day longer. The first-class postage rate also applies to all countries of the European Community. All intra-European mail goes by air. Air and surface rates are available to the United States and Canada. Parcels and packets should have a customs sticker (available from post offices).

Incoming mail can be addressed *poste restante* (general delivery) to main towns. It will then be available for collection at the main post office. Don't send *poste restante* parcels to other than a substantial town.

CONDITIONING. You don't have to be an Olympic athlete to follow these routes. How far and how fast you ride is up to you. Some days you might ride 20 miles in an hour, other days you mightn't ride a mile in 20 minutes, preferring instead to dabble your feet in a stream.

But it stands to reason that you do need some physical fitness. A regular program of cycling so that you can tackle 30 miles in a day in comfort will prepare you beautifully. If you can ride farther, so much the better.

Grass track racing is a regular feature of the second day of each summer's York Rally.

Be prepared for occasional tough climbs—usually short but occasionally of a mile or more. In the Aches in the Lakes ride, you do need to be physically fit; the big hill is tough for pushing a bike, let alone pedaling.

WEATHER AND SEASONS. Be prepared for weather that can change by the hour. Britain doesn't have Californian consistency. In the south, summer temperatures can rise to 80 degrees, although 75 is more normal. They can fall in winter to freezing. North of Manchester, temperatures are three or four degrees colder all year than on the south coast. In Scotland and along the northern English hills, it can often snow while the rest of the country enjoys sunshine.

The prevailing wind is from the west, which makes rainfall higher in the west than in the east. It can rain one day in three (although not usually all day!) in the west any time of year (end-of-year and August are the wettest months everywhere), but only a third as often along the east coast. East winds along the eastern edge of the country are biting cold in winter.

Apart from that, weather is much as you'd expect it—cheerful in spring, pleasant in summer, mellow in fall, and bleak in the winter.

WHAT TO TAKE

MONEY. The basic unit is the pound, written £, to which there are 100 pence. Since decimalization in the 1970s, penny has been shortened to "p" and you'll often hear it spoken that way—three pence as three-pee, for instance.

There are five national banks, plus Scottish and regional banks. All but minor branches sell or exchange travelers checks and change currency. The same applies to bigger travel agencies. Banks open principally from 10:00 A.M. to 3:30 P.M. weekdays, although the Trustee Savings Bank stays open later, and some banks open on Saturday mornings which are restricted to straightforward and relatively minor transactions. (Building societies aren't banks; they're money-lending organizations for house buyers.)

Britain is part of the Eurocheque system, and U.S. and Canadian checks aren't accepted. Ask advice of your bank before leaving. You can bring in as much currency as you wish.

Several banks issue currency notes. Bills from the Bank of England are legal tender in England, Wales, Scotland, the Isle of Man, Northern Ireland and the Channel Isles. Money from Scottish banks (such as the Clydesdale) are legal tender in Scotland and usually accepted elsewhere. Manx and Channel Islands money is valid only on those islands. Notes from Northern Ireland are valid there but occasionally accepted elsewhere.

Ireland (i.e., southern Ireland) is a separate nation and its money isn't legal tender in Britain. Nor is an Irish pound, or *punt*, worth £1 sterling.

Credit cards are used widely in Britain. American cards might be viewed with suspicion but should be accepted if they're MasterCard or Visa. MasterCard is known in Britain as Access; Visa is occasionally called Barclaycard. American Express is well known, Diner's Club less so. Shops and hotels display emblems of cards they accept.

BIKES AND RELATED GEAR. You don't need a super-whizz bike for these trips, but you will need two things: low gears and fenders. You'll regret leaving either behind. Get your bike shop to confirm that you have a bottom gear of 35 inches—no more than 45 inches even if you're an Olympic-level racer.

Apart from that, you'll need no more than you'd need for similar rides at home. Remember, though, that you need a white front lamp and a red rear lamp that meet British legal specifications; you can buy them without difficulty in the first town you reach, although the fact is that any bright, reliable light that you'd use without worry at home will most likely be suitable in Britain.

Take sufficient tools to mend flats and, if you can, replace a spoke and adjust brakes. A spare brake and gear cable is advisable in the Aches in the Lakes ride.

Why Bath is called Bath; this is where the Romans bathed, a view gazed over by the cathedral.

One day, someone will standardize tire sizes. Until then, sizes in the United States, Britain and continental Europe will differ. You will find the British sizes available in all British bike shops and in some nonspecialists, such as shops which also sell car spares. The metric sizes are available in most specialist bike shops and occasionally elsewhere. If you cross to continental Europe, you will find only the metric sizes, although, if you have one, a British 26-inch rim will usually double for a continental 700.

The only sizes given are those which have an equivalent in either British or metric. But since the situation is so confusing, the advice of a good bike shop is invaluable. The commonest sizes in Britain are marked in bold.

BRITISH	METRIC	AMERICAN
27 x 1		27 x 1$\frac{1}{8}$
27 x 1$\frac{1}{8}$		27 x 1$\frac{1}{4}$
27 x 1$\frac{1}{4}$		27 x 1$\frac{3}{8}$
	700 x 18C	**700 x 19C**
	700 x 22C	**700 x 25C**
	700 x 25C	**700 x 28C**

CLOTHING. Take with you clothes for cycling in—shorts are usually fine in summer but you'll need tracksuit bottoms as an alternative in other seasons. Casual dress is acceptable anywhere in Britain, but remember that you'll need warm clothing after sundown, regardless of the season. Keep a pair of tennis shoes handy for walking tough hills or exploring cathedrals and old houses.

Be sure to bring waterproof clothing in which you can cycle. A traditional cycling cape is fine—you can buy one at any British bike shop if you don't have one—but if you have several hundred dollars to spare, you could treat yourself to a rain suit made of fabrics which expel sweat but repel raindrops.

SURVIVAL SKILLS

This is the hodgepodge of information which makes your stay more enjoyable. It's a short-cut to background information that might take you several days or weeks to acquire otherwise.

SECURITY. Theft is a problem in Britain as elsewhere. Generally, your bike will be safe if you leave it briefly in all but city areas. But why take the risk? A bike stolen on a normal day is inconvenient; a bike laden with baggage, stolen on vacation, is disastrous. Lock it and, if necessary, remove the front wheel and lock it to the frame.

Check your insurance policy before you leave. If your bike is stolen, make sure you know the contact address for your insurance company. And tell the police—either by visiting the nearest police station or by dialing 999 (no coins needed). Sadly, there's little the police can do, but telling them might be a condition of your policy.

ROAD SAFETY. British roads are classified with Teutonic enthusiasm down to the smallest field path. Here they're described from biggest to smallest.

MOTORWAYS equate roughly to interstates. They're always what the British call dual carriageways (opposing traffic is separated by a grass or fence barrier called the central reservation) and they have limited access and exits. Motorways bear the prefix or suffix "M." So you might come across the M1 or the A1(M). There's a difference but it's not important. What matters is that you can't bicycle on them, and you probably wouldn't want to anyway.

CONVENTIONAL ROADS are graded A for the most significant, B for regional and C for district. A ring road is a circuit of roads, signed as such, which circles a town center or even an entire town, keeping traffic out of the downtown area. The main roads out of town radiate from the center and cross the ring road. In other words, it's a continuous bypass.

Most **A-roads** are fine for short distances or getting somewhere quickly, but some (like the A1) are motorways in all but name. Any A-road that's also a dual carriageway will usually be busier and faster (up to 90 mph, although the limit is 70) than you'd like. Main highways on which cycling is allowed are signed in green with yellow lettering.

B-roads can also be busy, especially in the southeast, because they link villages and small towns. But traffic is slower and the roads usually more rural. Outside the London area, you can often ride comfortably for hours on B-roads.

C-roads are usually a delight. They're also characteristically British because you have to know they're C-roads, since the letter and the number are rarely given. Only in parts of the county of Lincolnshire have I seen the number of C-roads posted (the numbers repeat every few miles, anyway, like the departmental roads of France). You can cross Britain on C-roads and never see more than a large village. The routes in this book are mostly on C-roads.

Surfaces are usually poorer, although always hard. There usually are no sidewalks (UK—pavement) or lighting outside villages, and usually no central white line. C-roads twist for no obvious reason, adding miles to your journey, but they're fun. Usually they'll be wide enough for cars to cross with caution, but sometimes they can be single tracks. In remotest Scotland, even A-roads can be single for miles.

Beware, though—country lanes are often cart tracks which have sunk below the surrounding fields. They twist around the boundaries of vanished fields, so you might ride for miles with limited vision. They're far from dangerous, but you need to get used to them.

Gradients in Britain are usually referred to in proportions. One-in-eight means one foot vertically for every eight horizontally. That's much the same as 12 percent and, increasingly, you'll see grades expressed in percentages. This is under the influence of the European

Community (most of Europe uses percentages) but hasn't yet permeated common British understanding. Of those you're likely to encounter: one-in-five equals 20 percent, one-in-six equals about 16 percent, one-in-seven equals about 14 percent, one-in-eight equals about 12 percent, one-in-ten equals 10 percent.

Off-road riding also presents good opportunities, if somewhat complicated by rights of way. You have the right to walk or cycle on any surfaced road in Britain that doesn't have an "M" in its number or isn't obviously a private road to, for example, a farm or remote house. On top of that, you have the right to cycle on some unsurfaced paths and tracks. This is complicated and, if you get it wrong, as likely to cause distress as it might in your own country. It's additionally complex because there is little case law to define the fringes of access law, and also because the law in England and Wales differs from the law in Scotland.

In England and Wales, paths and tracks are defined as follows (and in each case this is the established ruling):

Footpath (shown on the Ordnance Survey [OS] map as · · · · ·). Footpaths are for walkers. You may not cycle, but you can push your bike. By law, paths should be "wide enough for two men to pass without argument," but in practice many are neglected, overgrown or even

Freshwater, gateway to the Tennyson Trail

plowed out of existence. But whether the path is visible or not, you have the right to use it. There is a right of way when the $\cdots\cdots$ on the map is marked in red. There isn't an *absolute* right if it's in black. The right of way exists only where the map shows it to be—even if that's through the middle of crops. You (and the farmer) might prefer to walk the edge of the field, avoiding the central path, but technically that's trespass.

Trespass is a civil offense; you can be brought to court (although it's unlikely) to pay for whatever damage you caused. If you leave a gate open and let sheep stray on a busy road, the damage could be considerable; in practice, it's unlikely to be more than a few bent pieces of grass.

If you unintentionally end up trespassing, (a) smile and be courteous; (b) ask to be redirected to the legal route; and (c) be prepared to leave by whichever route the landowner asks. Remember, though, that the occasional farmer likes to think a path's not there even when it is.

Bridleways are a superior footpath, usually broader, sometimes the remnants of old cart roads. Some are delightful. You may cycle on a bridleway provided you show preference to walkers and horse riders. Drivers may also use bridleways if the path leads to land to which they need access. The sign for a bridleway is - - - - - - - - - . The same advice regarding rights of way and trespass on footpaths applies to bridleways, and the same rule that the bridleway has to be shown in red, not black.

A road used as a public path, known unattractively as a **Rupp,** is the next stage up. Some are promoted bridleways and there's little difference in appearance between a broad bridleway and a Rupp. The cycling organizations object to this uprating, though, because it allows access to everyone. It's unlikely you'll come across cars, heavy trucks and whatever else, but you might find trail-riding motorcyclists. A Rupp is shown as $\cdot$ - - - - - - - - - - and the above warnings apply.

Finally comes a rare beast called the **byway open to all traffic,** which is much the same thing as a Rupp. It's marked + $\cdot$ + $\cdot$ + $\cdot$ + $\cdot$.

If this sounds complicated, it amounts to this: you can ride any route on the Ordnance Survey map of England and Wales, provided it's not colored blue; it's not a footpath; it's not an obvious private access; or there isn't a specific exclusion sign. You can get a booklet on rights of way in England and Wales called *Out in the Country* from the Countryside Commission, at 19-23 Albert Road, Manchester M19 2EQ (061-224 6287).

Horse riders and walkers form a strong lobby in Britain, just as they do elsewhere. While cyclists have a right to be on these paths, it's only fair to say that there is growing resentment. Usually you will find nothing but courtesy and understanding. Nevertheless, Alan Harlow, the head of the Cyclists' Touring Club, the national body which repre-

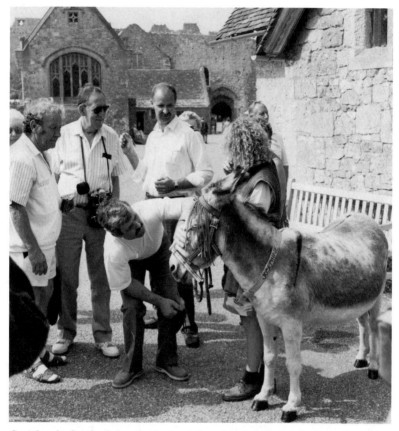

Carisbrooke Castle: Jenny the donkey takes a break from duty in the well wheel.

sents the leisure interests of British cyclists, has said that if a small group of mountain-bikers persists in acting inconsiderately and riding where they have no right, before long the time will come when off-road riding comes under the same pressure as elsewhere.

Some general rules of the road: Traffic travels on the left. Overtake only on the right, except in slow traffic or on one-way streets. To left turn, extend your left arm horizontally. It's not permissible to turn left against a red light. To turn right, check overtaking traffic, extend your right arm, move to the center of the road, ride to the junction, and turn right.

Unless signed otherwise, you have right of way while continuing on the major route. You do not have right of way where a white line crosses the road, as at a junction or a roundabout (circulatory junction). You can ride on all surfaced roads (other than obviously private ones) except those with an "M" in their number.

At night, you must have a red rear light, a red rear reflector and a white front light. The reflector can be combined with the rear lamp lens. Flashing warning lights are not allowed.

Wear a helmet if you'd normally ride in one at home. Helmet wear is less widespread in Britain than on the other side of the Atlantic, but it's increasing.

ACCIDENTS. It's not necessary to call the police to an accident, but you should if there's an injury. An injury or damage must, in any case, be reported to the police as soon as possible. Dial 999 for major cases; report to the nearest police station within a few hours for lesser accidents. It's always wise to ask for the other person's insurance details. These must be given by law. Drivers must have third-party insurance; cyclists don't. See also Health.

Call 999 for an ambulance. For less serious treatment, seek a hospital with an emergency department (usually in the nearest town). For a doctor or dentist ask locally.

INFORMATION, PLEASE. British newspapers get more serious as they get bigger. The Times (politically right), *Independent* (neutral), *Daily Telegraph* (right) and *The Guardian* (left) are the heavies. The *Sun* and *Star*, with their topless pin-ups, and the *Daily Mirror*, are down-market. *The Sport* or *Sunday Sport* are akin to the *National Enquirer* (now on sale in Britain).

There are also regional evening and morning papers, including Scottish dailies and local weeklies.

The BBC provides five national radio services: Radio 1 (pop), Radio 2 (sweet music), Radio 3 (classical), Radio 4 (speech) and Radio 5 (sports, education). All except Radio 5 are available on FM. Radio 5 is on medium-wave AM. Radio 4 is also on 198kHz long-wave.

Radio 4 provides world and national news hourly, with news programs from 6:30 A.M. to 8.45 A.M., 1:00 P.M. to 1:40 P.M., 5:00 P.M. to 6:30 P.M. and 10:00 P.M. to 10:30 P.M. weekdays. There are weather forecasts just before the hour in the breakfast, lunchtime and late-afternoon periods. Radio 4 also provides plays, humor, documentaries and current affairs analyses.

World news is available in eastern and southern England on the BBC World Service on 648kHz—not everywhere because the transmitters point to mainland Europe.

There are also 120 local stations, provided by the BBC or commercial companies. The BBC tends to speech, the commercials to pop. All give local, national and world news and local weather. And, as I write this, licenses have been given for national commercial stations.

There are four television networks. BBC-1 and Channel 3 (ITV) are entertainment channels. News is at 6:00 P.M. and 9:00 P.M. on BBC-1, at 5:45 P.M. and 10:00 P.M. on Channel 3. BBC-2 and Channel 4 are more specialized, with an emphasis on arts and documentaries. Channel 4 has hour-long news at 7:00 P.M. Satellite television is less developed; cable television is almost unknown.

TELEPHONES. Telephones are operated by British Telecom and its smaller rival, Mercury. Kiosks take coins or, sometimes, phone-cards (available from post offices and shops, but only for one network or the other).

Dial 999 for emergency help from the police, ambulance, fire brigade or coast guard. The service is free.

All international calls except Ireland start 010. For the United States or Canada, dial 010-1 followed by the area code (without any initial "0") and the desired number. Some kiosks—usually at London rail termini—accept credit cards.

Internal calls have an area code (known as the STD code) followed by the subscriber's number. Use the area code only if you call from one town to another. At Easter 1994, all STD codes will acquire an extra number, a 1, to make the phone network larger. For example, Norwich is now 0603 and will become 01603; Newcastle is 091 and will become 0191. The numbers in this book are the pre-1994 codes.

LANGUAGE. Everybody in Britain speaks English, although often with a strong accent. Glaswegian, Belfast and Tyneside (Newcastle) are sometimes all but incomprehensible to other British people. Gaelic, in different versions, is spoken in parts of Wales, Scotland and southern Ireland. Gaelic speakers also speak English, although not always as their first language.

Thanks to imported films and TV, the British are accustomed to many Americanisms. But here are ten things you might not have known . . .

A *flat* in your tire is a *puncture* in Britain. A flat is what you call an apartment.

A *bum* is what you sit on; a guy who sleeps rough is a *tramp*. And don't talk about your *fanny*, especially if you're female. It has a very different meaning.

The British swear as much as anyone, and often as vilely. But be careful about using what, in polite company, they call the "F-word." It's very offensive.

Water comes from a *tap*, not a *faucet*. It's kept off your *trousers* (pants) by *mudguards*, not fenders. And when you've accumulated too much, ask for the *toilet* or the *"loo"* (a corruption of Waterloo) and never for the restroom or comfort station, which will have your British friends rolling in mirth. You'll also get a smile of recognition of national stereotyping when you respond "You're welcome." The British don't say it automatically and its absence shouldn't be taken as an insult.

A *fag* is a cigarette, not slang for homosexual; and a *faggot* is a meatball made of offal. A *butt*, unless you make it clear, is a bucket for rainwater. And an *ass* is a donkey; it's vulgar to British ears, but your ass is our *arse*.

Almost no proper name is pronounced the way it's written. Warwick is Worrick; Leicester is Lester. The county of Norfolk (Nor-f'k) is rich in bizarre pronunciations—Happisburgh is Haze-br'; Wymondham is Winn-d'm; Costessey is Cossee. Almost all names in Wales are impossible to the English.

If you say something *bombed*, for most people here it means an explosive success.

If I do something well and you say it's "quite good," I shall be offended. To British ears, it's damning with faint praise. "Quite" usually equates to "moderately."

A *skillet* is a frying pan; cleats that grip your pedals are *shoeplates*; the stuff you spread on bread is *jam*, not jelly (which is what kids eat at parties); and soft drinks made from flavored syrup and water are called *squash*.

Folding money is a *note*, not a bill; we wait in *queues*, not lines . . . and so it goes on.

Differences you'll find in cycling are:

Cleats	=	Shoeplates
Clincher	=	Wired-on tire
Crankarms	=	Cranks
Drafting	=	Sitting in
Miss-and-out	=	Devil-take-the-hindmost
Paceline	=	Bit-and-bit
Seat post	=	Seat pin
Sew-ups	=	Tubulars (or "tubs")
Shifter	=	Gear change
Spinning	=	Twiddling
Wrench	=	Spanner (unless it's adjustable, in which case it's often called a wrench)

CYCLING CLUBS. The Cyclists Touring Club is a good source of information on everything to do with cycling. It's at 69 Meadrow, Godalming, Surrey (0483-417217), near Guildford, about an hour and a half's ride southwest of London. The Mountain Bike Club (0842-812359 or 0273-696054) is another good source.

TRANSPORTATION TO AND IN BRITAIN

I suppose people still sail to Britain on liners, clinking martini glasses and squabbling over who'll sit with the captain. But not many are bike riders.

So you'll fly. Don't worry too much where to. London's the obvious, but if you can get to Birmingham or Manchester or Glasgow for a great deal less, go there instead. The only consideration is that Glasgow (transatlantic flights are finally being transferred to Glasgow from Prestwick, which is on the coast near Ayr, about 40 miles away) leaves you in just the right place to see Scotland or northern England, but you're 400 miles north of London. Manchester is 250 miles north and Birmingham just 100.

If you want to see most of England, Birmingham's a good place to leave from because within miles you're into leafy lanes (although Birmingham itself is spiritless and dedicated to making and driving cars).

You'll have no trouble escaping from Glasgow, Birmingham or Manchester airports. Just follow the signs. London airports are trickier. Heathrow is the size of the biggest U.S. airports and as busy.

GETTING OUT OF HEATHROW. Little in life is more difficult than cycling out of Heathrow—not because it's dangerous (although there are safer hobbies and the roads inside and outside the airport are crowded) and not because it's impossible. It's simply complicated.

Bearing in mind that construction crews are forever digging up airports, here's how it's supposed to be when the pick-and-shovel brigade aren't at work.

From Terminals 1, 2 and 3. These are the terminals actually inside the airport, surrounded by runways. There is a Tourist Information office within the airport, near the Underground (subway) station.

To leave the airport, look for the general exit signs toward the north, which is the main direction out. Remember that the main road tunnel is banned to cyclists, so look for **cycle-path signs** on your left, pointing to a **special tunnel.** Take this tunnel and you'll emerge near the **Newport Road roundabout** near the busy A4 road which runs to London in one direction and Slough, Reading and (eventually) Wales in the other.

You are now 20 miles west of the city. There's no comfortable route into London, so take the **A4,** a straight and busy road, but safe enough and provided in parts with cycle paths (which are optional, which is as well, since the surface is poor and local people use them as parking lots).

From Terminal 4. Terminal 4 is outside the runway area, on the southeastern side. That makes it easier. Leave the terminal, bear right and follow signs for London and the A30. Turn left on the **A30** and follow that and, after a few miles, the **A4** to London. Or you can take a slightly less hectic route . . .

The quieter way is this: turn **right** instead of left on the **A30** so that you're going toward Staines. In less than 1 mile, you'll reach the **junction** with the A315 in a suburb called East Bedfont. Turn **left** and follow the **A315,** which is an old Roman road and therefore pretty straight, all the way through Hounslow to Brentford, where eventually it joins the A4 at a large **roundabout** 5 miles from the city center. Turn **right** on the **A4** and on no account get yourself up on the elevated section to the left (the M4), which is banned to cyclists.

Just before this junction, you might get your first glimpse of the Thames, to the right. If you turn right over Kew Bridge immediately after seeing the Thames, you'll get to the Royal Botanic Gardens.

It's not, unfortunately, possible to ride into London alongside the Thames.

From Terminals 1, 2 and 3 to Terminal 4. To get from Terminal 1, 2 or 3 to Terminal 4 is a ride of 4 miles. Follow the exit signs to the point near the radar tower. Watch for signs to the cycle path on your left (the road tunnel is banned to cyclists). Follow the cycle **path** through the **tunnel,** bear **left** on the **slip-road** and then **left** on **Northern Perimeter Road West.** Follow it round the eastern end of the airport and look for signs to Terminal 4.

To ride from Terminal 4 to the other terminals is also 4 miles, of course. Turn **left** from the terminal, then take the **signed route** round the eastern end of the airport. Turn **right** following the exit sign and go straight on at **Nene Road (roundabout)** to the A4. Turn **left** to **cross the motorway** and re-enter the airport at the next traffic light. Follow the **cycle path left** at the **next roundabout,** through the **special tunnel** to the central area.

By Train from Heathrow. There is a subway from Heathrow to Lon-

Newport, capital of the Isle of Wight; this is St. James' Square.

don, but unless you're lucky, you can't take a bike. Sometimes you can get on if the bike's still folded from the journey and the officials feel benevolent or sleepy. The trains are small and crowded, though, and your bike is unlikely to be popular. The subway service is all run by London Underground, but there are eleven interconnecting lines and two sizes of train, each with different rules about bikes. The best way to get information on all London subway services is by calling a London number, 071-222 1234 (24 hours).

Look at a map of the subway and you'll see each line is a different color (although the trains themselves are always red or silver and red). You can take a bike on the Metropolitan (purple), District (green) and Circle (yellow) lines anytime on weekends or public holidays, and from Monday to Friday between 10:00 A.M. and 4:00 P.M. and after 7:00 P.M. Expect to pay about half-fare for your bike.

(Just to amuse you, when the British say subway they don't mean a train but a subterranean pathway; subway trains in London are signed "Underground" but always called the Tube. In Glasgow, where the subway trains are so tiny that you look for a clockwork key in the side, they're just called the Underground.)

GETTING OUT OF GATWICK. . . . is relatively simple, because it's newer and in the country. Follow the exit signs, but not those for the M23 or other motorways. Cycling from Gatwick to London doesn't have many laughs, but there's a train. You can take a bike free and it doesn't have to reserved or folded—but see the section on Traveling by Train.

Trains leave every 15 minutes, less frequently by night, and take around half an hour, arriving at Victoria (one of several city-center termini), near Buckingham Palace. The single fare is around $10, but some tour operators can arrange a discount. In the opposite direction, trains to Gatwick leave platform 14, and the British Airways city check-in center is alongside it. There are also—but less frequently—direct trains from Gatwick to southern and mid-England, without changes in London.

Within Britain, you can generally get information on British Rail by visiting a main station or by calling 071-730 3400, which is the British Rail Travel Centre at 12 Regent Street, in London's West End. There's also a recorded announcement about the Gatwick Express, call 071-928 2113.

GETTING OUT OF STANSTED. Stansted (40 miles north of London) is London's third airport but still has the air of a wartime airfield that's found itself in an aviation boom. Its attraction to airlines is that it's cheap, and you're likely to land there if you cross by one of those airlines on which you provide your own sandwiches. But don't be put off—they're spending $750 million on improving it so that it'll handle up to 8 million passengers a year. Before modernization, it had 1.3 million, mostly travelers on organized vacations to Spain and Greece.

It's simple to cycle out of Stansted—just ¹/₂ mile to conventional roads and a little more before you're into byways. You can also use the new railroad directly to Liverpool Street station in eastern central London (40 minutes), to Cambridge, and elsewhere. As at Gatwick, the station is part of the airport.

Stansted is best if you want to start your tour in East Anglia (the stumpy eastern peninsula that includes Norwich, Cambridge and Constable Country—the area of Essex named after the landscape painter John Constable).

GETTING OUT OF LUTON. London is also served by a fourth airport, at Luton. It's on the edge of a charmless town (another car factory base) 30 miles north of London. Just follow the exit signs. It's a fast downhill all the way to Luton, from where there are trains to London, Birmingham and the English Midlands. Turn off in the other direction, though, and you're soon into quiet lanes which will take you all the way to the outskirts of the capital.

TRAVELING BY TRAIN. Britain has fast, frequent and moderately reliable trains, although line closures in the 1960s mean trains run mainly in and out of London and between major cities. Until the closures, you could steam past meadows and long-forgotten stations where the staff kept goats and were rarely troubled by passengers.

The fastest services run at up to 150 mph and few trains average less than 40 mph unless they're all-station-stoppers. In general, bikes travel free. But since nothing aggravates the British cyclist more than negotiating British Rail, I'll tell you now that although traveling by rail is a superb way of crossing the country, the restrictions are so varied and so often changed that you need a law degree to figure them all out.

The principle is that your bike can go free and unbooked on all trains except the fastest main lines, services in and out of London in the same direction as the rush hour, trains to Dover, Folkestone and sometimes Harwich which connect on the quayside with ferries, trains on the Isle of Wight, and . . . well, the list goes on.

On some you can't take a bike at all. On others you can sometimes and not others. On still others you can if you book and provided there aren't already two bikes there before you. None of this is helped by the confusion of British Rail staff and by the complexity of their booklet, *British Rail Guide to Better Biking* (available by mail and from larger stations). Even the booklet can be varied locally at the whim of staff.

But if all this puts you off, don't let it. Distances are too short and airline fares so high that the train is best. You can check the rules, and BritRail and other concessions, by calling or writing to British Rail locally. (See the appendix for addresses.) Call the local station the previous day, follow the rules for the train you want, and arrive about 15 minutes before departure. Tie a label to your bike, naming its final destination, and load it in the baggage car (known as the guard's van).

There's just more than a 50 percent chance that this will be toward the end rather than the front of the train—it's a normal passenger car (UK—carriage) with a freight area and an attendant (the guard). Fix your bike to something solid with a toestrap, but never lock it to anything. If you do, tons of mail will smother your bike because the guard couldn't move it.

Many of the routes in this book can be linked by train (or by a cycling route, given at the end of each ride for which this is possible). You can also take the train from London to the start of each route; the rail information is given in the information block at the beginning of each route.

LONDON. Cycling in London is no more dangerous than riding in any other big city. Plenty of people do it every day, and you'll see them with grime and sweat-streaked faces, never smiling, always concentrating on the traffic.

Frankly, I don't think it's worth cycling in London at all if you're there to enjoy yourself. The tourist attractions (Piccadilly, Oxford Street, Tower Bridge and so on) are all within a couple of square miles. And while the Underground can be pretty tedious and frequently crowded, it's safe and it's predictable. You might spend more time riding the escalators than riding the trains, but you don't have to leave your bike locked outside every place you want to visit.

Most of the attractions are on the north side of the Thames, which is where the Underground serves best. There are all-day tickets, but there are no leave-your-bike services at Underground stations. Check the section on Transportation to and in Britain for information on which Underground trains will take your bike.

London has an intensive public bus service, with double-deckers on most routes. Usually you pay the driver as you enter. This makes the bus hopelessly slow. It's also confusing, even to locals, because the sign on the bus gives only the sketchiest information where the bus is passing through.

If you do want to cycle in London, you can cross the Thames at any of the bridges. Of the few tunnels, you must wheel your bike through the Greenwich and Woolwich pedestrian tunnels (it takes longer but it's more fun to use the Woolwich ferry); there is a motorized ferry service through the Dartford-Purfleet tunnel (report at the tunnel offices at the entrance); and if you enjoy nervous exhaustion and gaseous intoxication, you're free to cycle through the Rotherhithe tunnel if you wish. You can't cycle through the Blackwall tunnel.

THE OPEN ROAD

For such a small country, there's an awful lot of Britain. Don't be confused about places seeming close together. Traveling in Britain shouldn't be hurried. Don't fool yourself that you're going to "do" ev-

*Ryde, the Isle of Wight: a busy little town with ferry connections and plenty of
places to eat and stay.*

Easy-going pastoral riding in the Vale of York; this is a group enjoying themselves at the annual York Rally.

erywhere from the Scottish islands down to the Scilly Isles in 2 weeks, because you're not. You couldn't do it even if you drove hard between selected areas. And anyway, what's the point of trying?

The routes are samples of Britain. But let's come to this understanding: there are so many subtle variations within just a few miles and I could make so many suggestions that it would take the Pentagon computer to absorb them all. I've picked one or two in each of my favorite areas. They're not the only ones, but they're good ones. On top, I suggest optional side rides, because there's something interesting just off the route.

By the time you've made one or two of the extra journeys, and taken your time on the routes themselves, each circuit could take two or three days. Alternatively, you could do most of them in a day if you enjoy athletic challenges more than seeing the countryside.

There's a lot more that I could have included but didn't. The Peak District between Sheffield and the Scottish border is magnificent, but you won't find it here. Since I couldn't get everything in, I left it out because it's too hilly. The same applies to Cornwall and to all but the Welsh borders.

You'll find Oxford but you won't find Cambridge; the city's fine but the countryside is undistinguished.

The neighboring Fens aren't here because they're as flat as Florida (but with neither crocodiles nor sun) and as empty as the prairies. Northern Scotland's not here because you don't need a route guide to Northern Scotland—everywhere's beautiful and there aren't many roads either.

I didn't tell you about Windsor because the town's better than the countryside, which is now largely commuter villages, computer companies and out-of-town supermarkets. I also haven't mentioned the immediate surroundings of Birmingham, the area east and northeast of London, the peninsula between Manchester and Liverpool, and much of Glasgow's outlying areas; I think of them as embarrassing relatives—obligation forces us to acknowledge each other but I find it hard to strike up a friendship.

I hope you'll be able to follow each section without a map, although I suggest you don't. The ground rules are simple. First, where it's obvious which road you stick to at a junction (be it through signposting, lines on the road or whatever), I don't mention the direction unless it makes matters clearer. If in doubt, follow the marked or major way.

Second, I don't say north or south. The road network is too dense, the junctions too imprecise, and country lanes too likely, as Shakespeare put it, to roll like an English drunkard. I say left, right, or whatever. Ask a local whether to turn north or south and all you'll achieve is bewilderment. We British aren't given to compass directions, firmly believing we're already at the world's center.

And third, these aren't "go-and-see" rides. Sure, sometimes I'll take you past some beautiful scene or an imposing relic. But there are few specifics. Instead, the countryside changes every dozen miles; you'll go through villages on and well off the tourist trail; you'll see the real Britain and you'll go home (I hope) loving the place.

And oh yes . . . one of the routes goes right by my front door. I'm not telling you which—but I'll be looking for you!

A Note About Safety

Safety is an important concern in all outdoor activities. No guidebook can alert you to every hazard or anticipate the limitations of every reader. Therefore, the descriptions of roads, trails, routes, and natural features in this book are not representations that a particular place or excursion will be safe for your party. When you follow any of the routes described in this book, you assume responsibility for your own safety. Under normal conditions, such excursions require the usual attention to traffic, road and trail conditions, weather, terrain, the capabilities of your party, and other factors. Keeping informed on current conditions and exercising common sense are the keys to a safe, enjoyable outing.

Political conditions may add to the risks of travel in Europe in ways that this book cannot predict. When you travel, you assume this risk, and should keep informed of political developments that may make safe travel difficult or impossible.

The Mountaineers

PART II

YOUR ROAD TO ENGLAND

Hundreds go to the York Minster cyclists' service and on the organized rides at the York Rally.

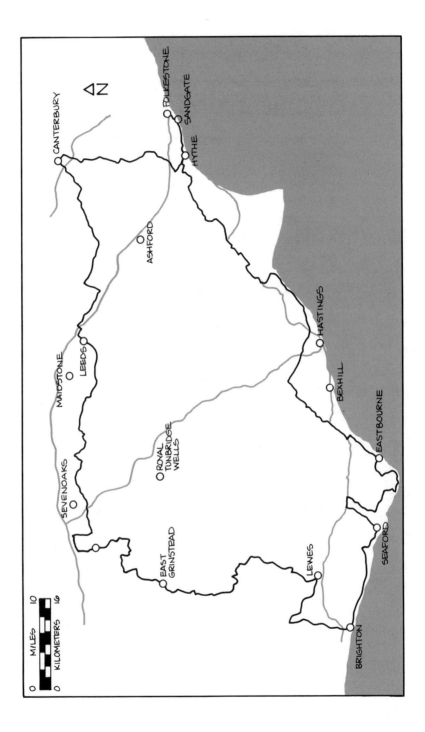

TOUR NO. 1

THE GARDEN OF ENGLAND
Kent and East Sussex

Distance: 230 miles

Estimated time: 5 riding days

Terrain: Moderate, with flat sections and a few stiff climbs

Maps: Ordnance Survey 179, 187, 188, 189, 198, 199

Rail: Maidstone has three stations served from London (ask British Rail which service suits you best); other stations on the route are served from Victoria, Charing Cross or Waterloo; all destinations are within about 1½ hours.

To people of Kent, who divide themselves into Men of Kent — east of the river Medway—and Kentish Men—to the west—only one area deserves the title "Garden of England." It is, you'll not be surprised, Kent. This multiday tour, though, loops through East Sussex as well, so I hope I'll be forgiven.

This is your instant initiation into gentle England. The southeast peninsula has warm villages, a good climate (in summer, but winters can be cold), rolling hills, village greens and ancient buildings.

In it, you'll see the fairy-tale castle of Leeds, follow the footprints of pilgrims to the mighty cathedral of Canterbury, ride two strange railroads (and possibly one rather dull one), visit Brighton and its Royal Pavilion, see the mysterious hillside chalk carving of Wilmington, pass the Battle of Hastings and visit Winston Churchill's lovely home at Chartwell.

The southeastern peninsula is indeed a garden. The area's dominated by two ridges—the North and South Downs. By Rocky Mountain standards they're pimples, but they shouldn't be underestimated. The fields are green and soft, or gold from corn, but the underlying chalk rears in swerves that'll have you sweating.

But then, to compensate, there's also the flat reach of Romney Marsh and its smuggling country; the British have always had a fondness for old-time smugglers, and romanticize and frequently make commercial capital from them.

If you don't want to ride the whole route, take the train from Lon-

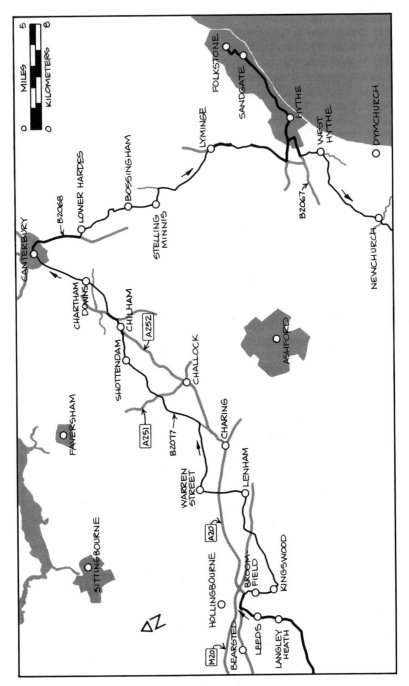

don to the start of any section and back from the end. The main train lines radiating from London cross the route repeatedly.

You can get details of cycling in Sussex from West Sussex County Council, Tower Street, Chichester PO19 1RL (0243-777420). Leaflets include a circular tour of the county, going further west than this route. There's a similar service from Kent County Council, Springfield, Maidstone ME14 2LL (0622-696165).

Leeds Castle to Canterbury and Folkestone: 49 Miles

This route starts at **Leeds Castle,** on the **A20** 5 miles east of **MAIDSTONE,** the county town of Kent.

Leeds is a medieval fairy-tale castle set in a lake. Many confuse it with Leeds in Yorkshire, but the name's a corruption of Led, the chief minister of Ethelbert IV, who was the king of Kent in 857. It was the favorite home of eight medieval queens and then became a palace for Henry VIII, who used it to escape the plague in London. It's open daily in summer and over Christmas, weekends in winter (0622-765400).

From the A20 going southeast toward Ashford, pass the castle grounds and a golf course, and then turn **right** into **a lane** ("Broomfield"). It's a relief to get off the A20, into a quiet lane with high hedges.

Go through **Broomfield** (2 miles), up through a straggle of houses. The lane brings you to the bungalow village of **Kingswood** 1 mile later, followed by a **junction.** Turn **left** into **Gravelly Bottom Road** ("Ulcombe, Lenham") and follow signs to **Lenham** (7 miles). Lenham's got a pretty central square with timber-framed and brick buildings. Very quaint and fine for coffee.

Go on to the **A20** and turn **right** ("Ashford"). Three-quarters of a mile later, turn **left** ("Warren Street, Otterden") to go up Hubbards Hill. This is quite a climb up to the ridge, along the edge of which runs the Pilgrims Way. Pilgrims walked this way to Canterbury in Chaucer's day, to the shrine of St. Thomas Becket ("who will rid me of this troublesome priest?" said Henry II in despair at the way the archbishop was resisting the monarchy's attempts on the clergy's privileges; four knights took the king's wish seriously and killed Becket on the cathedral steps in 1170—he was canonized two years later).

It's a **narrow road** through hedges. Go to the edge of **Warren Street** (10 miles) and take the **first right turn** into **Waterditch Road** ("Charing"), by the discreetly labeled Harrow Inn. Go along Waterditch Road, another hedged, narrow lane, but with restricted views ahead. It drops gently, still following the pilgrims' route. Go **straight ahead** at **all junctions.** The only one that might give you difficulty is at 12½ miles. Go straight over, into **Bowl Road** ("Stalisfield church, Throwley, Forstall"), and then immediately straight ahead outside the Bowl pub where the road swings right.

The restful beauty of Chartwell, where Churchill spent his life and became an American citizen.

Finally, the lane brings you (14 miles) to the unsignposted **junction** with the **B2077.** Turn **left** through **Longbeech Wood,** in and out of trees for several miles. Cross the **A251** to **Shottenden** (19 miles) and straight on to **Chilham.** The road then whooshes into the valley of the Great Stour down Soles hill. Take care—there's a **junction** at the bottom.

Turn **left** on the **A252** ("Ashford, Canterbury") and then immediately **right** into **Chilham** (24 miles). Apart from an unbelievable number of parked cars, Chilham is beautiful. There are Tudor and Jacobean timber houses, a single twisting road, a beautiful church, and the remains of a castle. There are also several restaurants. It'd be good to get here before everyone else.

Go through the village and down the hill. At the bottom, cut across to the **A252** on your left and turn **right.** The A252 becomes the **A28** and goes into the neighboring and distinctly less lovely village of **Bagham.**

The next turn is difficult to spot. It's at the far end of the village. First, on the right you'll see a turn for the railway station, then a succession of gas stations, car showrooms and a side street called

Meadow Close. Then you'll see a Fina gas station. Turn **right** alongside it into a **narrow unsignposted lane**.

Go through woods, over a river and up out of the valley on this narrow lane, so quiet that there's moss in the middle. It climbs between high hedges, swings left at the top at Mystole Farm and shortly afterward passes some converted oast houses. Oast houses, the symbol of Kent, were used to dry crops used in the preparation of beer. Few are still in use and most that survive have been converted into novel and not inexpensive houses.

This lane rears to the top of **Chartham Downs,** where there's a **crossroads.** Go across into **Chartham** (25 miles) and on into the outskirts of **CANTERBURY.** The Stour valley below you to the left is spoiled by factories, but a more famous sight awaits. Just after the 30 mph signs you'll get a snatched view ahead through the houses of Canterbury cathedral. The road then swings left and brings you to the **main road.** Turn **right** into Canterbury city center (29 miles).

Not for nothing is Canterbury famous. You'll appreciate a guidebook. There's the cathedral, of course (open daily; 0227-762862), the Christchurch Gate (where curfew is rung each night) and the restored Tudor cottages of The Weavers overhanging the Stour at King's bridge. Outside the Weavers Arms is a ducking stool. It warns: "Unfaithful wives beware . . . butchers bakers brewers apothecaries and all who give short measure . . ."

Southwest, on the banks of the Stour, is the 700-year-old church of Thanington Without—said to be the one that Thomas Gray described in his "Elegy Written in a Country Churchyard."

Leave Canterbury on the old **A2** toward Dover (in other words, don't get involved with the A2(T), the bypass which you crossed on the way in). Along the A2, and from the city's inner ring road, you'll see signs for the B2068 to Hythe. Take those directions and follow the **B2068** out of the city. We now go south for the coast.

Follow the B2068 to the **Lower Hardres** sign (32 miles), on for a farther ½ mile to a pub called the Granville, and turn **left** ("Lower Hardres, Upper Hardres, Bossingham"). There's not much to **Upper Hardres** except aristocratic permanency—it's been the home of the Hardres family since the Norman conquest. If you stop at the church, there's some rare 13th-century glass.

Follow signs to Bossingham (36 miles) and leave on the **Lyminge and Folkestone road**. You're now clear of the North Downs and the countryside is flatter. On the other hand, the South Downs follow in a few miles.

Follow signs to Lyminge, across the wooded common of **Stelling Minnis** (a good place for a picnic), down Longage Hill into **Lyminge** (42 miles) and on along the **B2065** to Hythe, dropping through the folds of the South Downs on a glorious descent. It's near here that the

Channel Tunnel starts and you'll see evidence of railway marshaling yards and new roads.

Go into **HYTHE** (47 miles), getting a glimpse of Hythe castle as you drop into the town. A sign tells you that this is one of the Cinque (say *sink*) ports. Until the 16th century, they were obliged to supply men and ships against invasion. The original ports were Hythe, Sandwich, Dover, Romney and Hastings; later came Rye and Winchelsea.

In the center, go **left** ("Sandgate, Folkestone") and then immediately **right** into **Twiss Road** ("To the sea"). Go to the end and it does indeed lead you to the sea. Turn **left** along the sea's edge toward **Sandgate.**

On a clear day you might make out sun glinting from the windshields of cars in France. Curiously, the tunnel which will start near the English Sandgate will emerge near Calais at Sangatte.

On the way to the seafront, you cross the Royal Military Canal for the first of several times. It's a pretty waterway now and in Hythe you

The Old Weavers at Canterbury—a gem from the Garden of England.

can rent a rowing boat to explore it. But once it was defensive, a moat to keep out the French.

Follow the **coast road** for 1½ miles, a golf course to your left, the sea to the right. At the **junction** with the **Hythe–Folkestone road,** turn **right,** still following the sea, into **SANDGATE** (49 miles).

Sandgate is a single road with shops and cafés, but it, too, was a defensive position. In the center is a Martello tower, a fez-shaped gun emplacement—again against the French. There are also the remains of a castle built by Henry VIII with the help of 900 men (contemporary details of how he and they did it are in the British Museum). The castle's now a private home, but it's open to visitors in summer (0303-221881).

Sandgate is a suburb of **Folkestone,** a Victorian resort and ferry terminal for France. The crossing takes 1½ hours. There is, though, a pleasanter way to Folkestone than along the main road (flatter, too, because the main road goes up a sudden hill after Sandgate).

Ride through Sandgate to the foot of the hill. You'll see stone steps to the right. They bring you to a **footpath** and then to a **toll road** (bikes go free) and on to the **garden seafront** of Folkestone, called **The Leas,** 200 feet above the sea. Much more enjoyable.

If you return to London by train, Folkestone Central station is on the inland side of the town, signposted from the center. If you stay, there are hotels in Folkestone, but in Sandgate you'd get a sea view for half the price.

Folkestone to Hythe and Hastings: 40 Miles

From **SANDGATE,** retrace on the **main road,** but instead of turning left at the **junction,** go **straight** ahead into **Hythe** (53 miles). At the **first roundabout,** take the **Hastings and Ashford exit** on the **A259,** alongside the canal.

Cross the canal and move to the **right** on the **one-way road** for the **exit** at the traffic lights signposted "Lympne and Sellindge." That takes you past the end of the Romney, Hythe and Dymchurch railroad. Those three towns are stations on the line—as is Dungeness, 14 miles farther on.

More remarkable is that the track is only 15 inches wide and that the steam engines are copies of mainline locomotives of the 1930s. They weigh nine and one-half tons and run at 20 mph. The line began in 1927 as a toy for the racing car driver Jack Howey but operates now for tourists. It runs all summer and some days in winter (0679-62353).

One of the stations is at Greatstone-on-Sea. Look for a series of vertical concrete dishes and walls, 25 feet high and 200 feet long. Boffins had the idea in 1928 that they might reflect the sound of enemy aircraft, a forerunner of radar. There weren't any enemy aircraft for eleven years, so nobody ever knew if they worked.

Pass Hythe station and leave on the **Ashford and London road,** still signed to Lympne and Sellindge. That takes you up a long hill away from the coast. At the top, turn **left** on the **B2067** ("Lympne"). The road goes sharply downhill and there's a fair bit of traffic; it's part of a popular coastal drive.

Lympne castle—the remains of a Roman fort—is ½ mile from here, signed ahead. The route, though, turns **left** at a **small stone cross** ("West Hythe, Dymchurch") down a steep hill between trees for ½ mile into West Hythe (57 miles), recrossing the canal to reach the flats of **Romney Marsh.**

This was smuggling country, the locals escaping across the marshes and drainage ditches. They knew the way; the excise men floundered. One of the most celebrated smugglers was a clergyman called, appropriately, Dr Syn.

The lane brings you to Botolphs Bridge—a **junction,** a pub and a bridge. Go over the bridge and follow signs to Newchurch. The road now is flat. It swings through sheep fields and around villages with quaint names: Ivychurch, Brookland, St. Mary-in-the-Marsh.

Go on to **Newchurch**, via a **staggered junction,** and into the village (63 miles). It's neat and pretty with a big stone church. At the **T-junction** beyond the church, turn **right** ("Bilsington, Ashford") and then, 50 yards farther, **left** to follow signs to **Ivychurch** (67 miles).

On the village outskirts, just before a pub and church, turn **right** ("Brookland, Rye, Hastings"). Pass Brenzett aeronautical museum (68 miles), cross the **A259** at **Brenzett** and follow signs along the **A259** to **Brookland** (69 miles) over Walland Marsh (less attractive than neighboring Romney Marsh) to **RYE** (76 miles).

No one would dispute this being one of Britain's most picturesque towns. The steep, cobbled lane of Mermaid Street is lined by houses from the 15th to 17th centuries, there's the old fort and prison of Ypres Tower, and the Quarter Boys clock of the parish church, where model boys strike the quarter hours but not the hours themselves.

At the **roundabout** by the cricket ground, turn **left** toward Hastings and continue by a beautiful white windmill and hundreds of sailing boats, round the river bridge staying on the **Hastings road,** to turn **left** on the far side of town to **Rye Harbour** (78 miles). Rye used to be on the coast, but the sea receded. Ships still call at Rye Harbour, as you'll detect from the industrial estate alongside the river.

This way skirts the coast rather than using the A259 on a hillier route inland. Go through Rye Harbour and on to where the road runs out, alongside a trailer park (79 miles).

There's a Martello tower at the end and, alongside it, the Frenchman's Beach caravan site. To the left of Frenchman's Beach is a **path** toward the coast. Push your bike along here and then round to the right at the end, across expanses of pebbles that harbor sea birds.

The road runs out at **Winchelsea Beach** (82 miles) and joins the

small road that links Winchelsea with the outskirts of Hastings (the original Winchelsea no longer exists: it fell into the sea in the 13th century). You can't see the sea from the Winchelsea Beach road because of a grassy bank. But if you take the steps, you'll find a stony beach populated by people escaping the razzmatazz of Hastings.

Ahead are the hills beyond which Hastings stands. Go that way, through **Pett Level** (83 miles). The road winds and rolls, with summer traffic, to **Fairlight** (85 miles). Now it's much hillier, getting you grabbing for your gears, but to the right there are occasional views of Brede Level, the floodplain of the river Brede.

The road reaches **Hastings** at 89 miles. If you turn left, you can zoom into Hastings, which has a pier, two stony beaches, cafés, hotels and all you'd expect of a vacation resort. It makes a pleasant break to watch the sea, but the climb back is long and arduous. There's a direct train service from Hastings to London but, as ever, check with British Rail about taking your bike.

Hastings to Eastbourne and Brighton: 53 Miles

From **Hastings**, turn **right** on the **A259** at the end of the **Fairlight road,** then **left** 50 yards later at traffic lights ("London, Battle") on the **B2093.** Follow signs to **Battle** (93 miles).

Battle Abbey celebrates the best-known date in English history: 1066. It was then that William the Conqueror, a French baron, defeated the travel-weary Harold II and his army and made the last successful invasion of England.

William built Battle Abbey to help local people celebrate the way he'd done them down. He'd promised God an abbey if He helped out. Quite how anybody knows is a puzzle, but the high altar is supposed to mark where Harold died from an arrow through his eye.

Battle Abbey—nothing's left aboveground of William's original building—is on your side of town as you enter. Go down the hill, **cross** the **railroad line** at Battle station and turn **left** on the **B2095** ("Catsfield"). The site of the Battle of Hastings is now on your right.

Turn **left** on the **A269** ("Bexhill") to **Catsfield** (95 miles) and **Ninfield** (97 miles). Then go **left** opposite the Kings Arms ("Bexhill, Hastings") and **right** soon afterward ("Pevensey"). Follow signs to **Pevensey** (104 miles), which is where William landed.

The last part of this road is dreary, across Pevensey Levels on the **A259,** but there's no worthwhile alternative. Pevensey has Tudor houses and shops and a castle (which was incomplete and unmanned when William invaded—he took it and gave it to a relative). Follow the A259 into **EASTBOURNE** (109 miles), taking the **seafront road.**

Eastbourne sees itself a cut above both Hastings (shabby) and Brighton (vulgar). Perhaps because it has more sun than anywhere in Britain, it attracts people who come to retire. It has, along with places

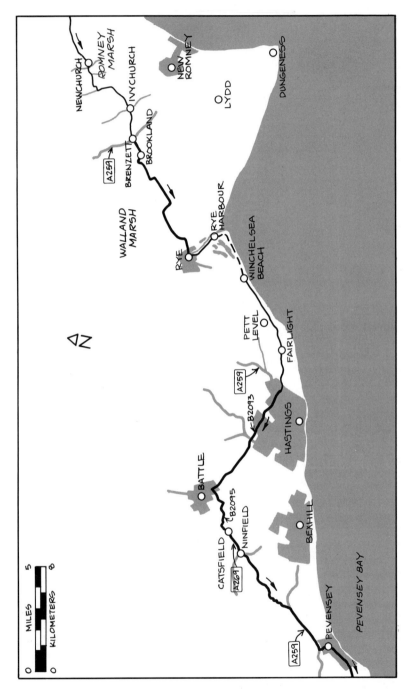

such as Worthing, a remarkably high average age. It has to make a living, though, so it advertises its beach and grassy banks in summer and its conference hall in winter.

Keep on past Eastbourne's bright white pier, and on along the seafront. When you get to the grassy gardens by the lifeboat museum, the road angles away from the beach and climbs. On your left you'll get your first glimpse of the white cliffs that make up Beachy Head and the Seven Sisters.

The climb gets harder, up by big houses with big gardens and up out of the town. Keep going, sometimes with difficulty, bending and twisting through trees, the road cutting around the hillside. Keep on at a give-way sign and take the **next lane left,** ¼ mile later, signposted Beachy Head.

Beachy Head is the most prominent of the chalky headlands that soar above the sea. At its base is a lighthouse. The land is open and green, farmed but with few fences. The sea shines and in a trick of geography you see it to both left and right as you climb.

When you get to the top (it's 550 feet from sea level in 1½ miles), you can walk to the edge and peer down (and wonder how the people sunbathing below got there). But take care: chalk is fragile and your weight might make it crumble and fall, with you following, hundreds of feet into the sea.

The Seven Sisters are farther rises between Beachy Head and the mouth of the Cuckmere. This coastline is now owned for the nation.

The descent is lovely, winding through green countryside, the clouds low above your head. The bottom comes at 115 miles, at **Birling Gap.**

If you like sea air (force-fed when the wind blows), take the **path** along the clifftop and down to Birling Gap. Otherwise make the same trip by **road.**

(If you come by mountain bike, there's a further chance for off-road riding, without unnecessary detours. Where the road swings back on itself, a path carries straight on. It runs over the Seven Sisters, then moves inland to meet the Cuckmere. Follow it to the A259 at Cuckmere bridge.)

If you go by road, round the hairpin and carry on to the **A259** at **East Dean** (116 miles). Turn **left** ("Seaford, Newhaven, Brighton"). You go up again straightaway, but not for long. The highest point gives you more views, over to Seaford and the more distant parts of the South Downs, the sea shining to the left. If you ever wondered what "meander" meant when applied to rivers, you'll understand when you see the Cuckmere twisting to the sea.

Turn **right** at the Cuckmere to Litlington. This is a diversion past the Long Man of Wilmington and through Alfriston, starting with Friston Forest, the broad Cuckmere valley to your left, the hills rising sturdily beyond it. Go through **Litlington** (121 miles) and then toward Wilmington.

One and a quarter miles on from Litlington, look over your right shoulder for the 226-foot-tall Long Man of Wilmington, carved into the hillside, legs apart, arms raised, a stave in each hand. Nobody knows how he got there. Just after the 30 mph signs as you enter Wilmington, a footpath takes you to the carving itself, but you'll get a better view from the road.

Go through **Wilmington** (124 miles), a pretty street of cottages of all shapes and colors, with attractive gardens. Reach the **A27,** turn **left** ("Lewes, Brighton") and ride 1 mile across the valley to a **roundabout.** Turn **left** down the other side to **Alfriston** (127 miles) with its clergy house and the winding street of stone, brick and half-timbered houses. It's best visited morning or evening because of the traffic.

The Clergy House is on the Tye, next to St. Andrew's church. It's a beautiful timber-framed house with a thatched roof and a tall, slender brick chimney. It was built for parish priests in the days when pilgrims still walked to Canterbury. It belongs to the National Trust and it's open from Easter to the end of October (0323-870001).

Once you clear the valley, you pay for good views with a long hill called the High and Over. The sea and the Downs come back into view, and straight ahead of you, **Seaford** (130 miles), another Cinque port.

Turn **right** on the **A259** and follow it 14 miles to Brighton. This is a dreary road—direct but a succession of disappointing towns and ribbon development. On the main road, you'll pass Seaford station; you could catch a train to Brighton.

(The railway takes a loop inland, so if you weren't bothered about Brighton and the first miles of the next section either, you could get off at Lewes, halfway from Seaford to Brighton, and rejoin from there.)

The road to Brighton isn't appalling, it's just unremarkable. It does, though, pass through **Newhaven.** You can take a one-day (or longer) trip from there to Dieppe. The crossing takes 4 hours; details from Sealink, the ferry operator (0273-514131). A mile west of Newhaven, you pass from the eastern hemisphere to the west, crossing the Meridian in the suburb of **Peacehaven.**

So, you reach **BRIGHTON** by road . . .

The marina on the outskirts houses 2,000 yachts, as well as the World War II destroyer *Cavalier*. On the town side is Brighton's famous naturist beach, of which it is both proud and embarrassed.

The Royal Pavilion is in the town center (142 miles). The Prince Regent built it as a dream palace and succeeded. It was finished in 1822 and much of the furniture's on loan from the Queen. It opens daily (0273-603005).

Brighton's most popular area, after the beach and the Pavilion, is The Lanes, the 17th-century cottage village of original Brighton. They have a charm, though they're ruined by tourism.

Brighton has a place in the hearts of the southern British, particularly Londoners. People who live there love it; those who visit say it isn't what it was. The truth is that Brighton, with its raciness and continental decadence, probably never *was* what it was. Graham Greene, who set *Brighton Rock* there, confessed that the Brighton of the book never quite existed—a fond concoction. And that sums it up best.

Those who regret its brassiness tend toward the dignified suburb of Hove. This gives it the soubriquet of Hove-actually:

"So you live in Brighton, do you?"

"Well, Hove actually."

Along the seafront in Brighton runs the Volk's Seafront Railway. It began when Brighton became a resort, in the Victorian era, in 1883. It's named after a local inventor, Magnus Volk, who used revolutionary electricity to power it. It runs along the top of the beach from the Aquarium, past the funfair to Brighton Marina, from Easter to October. Another curiosity is the National Museum of Penny Slot Machines, from an era when video games were unknown. It's on the seafront.

Brighton is about an hour from London by train. The station is signposted from the seafront.

Brighton to Battle and Chartwell: 58 Miles

From the Palace Pier, turn **right** in front of the Royal Albion hotel at a **roundabout** ("London, Gatwick, Lewes"). Shortly afterward you'll get to a large decorative church, with a war memorial across the road in front of it.

Go to the **left** of the church, take the **first right** round the back, and then **first left** (unsignposted) into **Ditchling Road.** Go straight ahead up the hill, due north. This is a long, long climb, with several false summits. The views improve as you ascend, but it's often spoiled by factories.

At a **staggered junction,** go **straight** ahead ("Ditchling"). This is the shallow side of **Ditchling Beacon.** The opposite way is the route of the London–Brighton bike rally, which began with half a dozen friends and now brings tens of thousands each summer. The countryside is open, green but with few trees or hedges. The hills roll in great hummocks.

The summit—Beacon Hills had bonfires to spread news of invasion by the Spanish—is at 150 miles. The views are remarkable. Take your time on the descent; it looks as though you can see half of southern England. The road dives and twists, with glimpses every so often of the countryside. At the bottom (152 miles), turn **right** on the **B2112** into **Ditchling** village. (If you wish to connect with the next tour, the Isle of Wight, this is your departure point. See the link at the end of this tour.)

If you were to turn left before the bottom of the hill, though, you'd

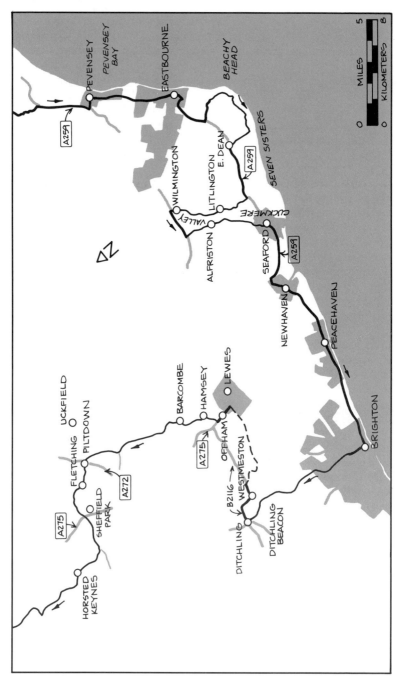

have come to the landmarks of the Jack and Jill windmills, near Clayton. Jack was made of brick in 1866. Jill is wooden and came to Clayton reluctantly; she was made in Brighton and then dragged to Clayton by oxen around 1850. The author and nonsense poet Hilaire Belloc used to live in the mills.

In Ditchling, turn **right** at the church on to the **B2116 (Lewes Road)** and follow through **Westmeston** (154 miles). The road swings left in the village. Half a mile later on the **left** is **Streat Lane,** to Streat, and immediately after it an unsignposted and unsurfaced path to the **right.**

Take that path. It swings right, then sharply left and up the steep side of the South Downs. There's a **crossroads** at the summit. Turn **left** and follow the path along the ridge to **LEWES** (158 miles), which you'll see below you a few miles farther.

If you prefer not to take this cross-country route, press on along the **B2116** and turn **right** on the **A275** into Lewes (say *Loo-iss*).

It's a town of narrow, steep streets with a castle in the center and dozens of interesting buildings. East of Lewes is Glyndebourne opera house, where audiences in evening dress enjoy outdoor music from May until August.

Leave Lewes on the **A275,** going north to **Offham** (159 miles). Turn **right** by the church ("Hamsey"). This **narrow lane** makes a change after the main road. **Hamsey** hardly exists, but there is a fork. Ignore the road to Cooksbridge and take the **right-hand lane,** then **left** at the **next fork** ("Barcombe Cross"), then **left** again at the **next fork,** basically going straight ahead.

Go into **Barcombe Cross** (162 miles). Turn **left** at the **small roundabout** ("Spithurst, Newick"), down the hill out of the village. You're now clear of the downs and it's easier going. The lane is still narrow. Where it bends, go straight on ("Piltdown").

At the **T-junction** at 167 miles, turn left ("Newick") and then immediately **right** ("Fletching"). Go over the **A272** into the attractive village of **Fletching** (168 miles). It's got an interesting gatehouse, church and half-timbered houses.

You're now entering the Ashdown Forest. It's many years since it was one continuous wood. Rather, like the New Forest, it's a lot of isolated woods.

Follow signs for **Sheffield Park** until you reach the **A275.** The 100-acre park by Capability Brown—famous for its rhododendrons and its five lakes at different levels—is left, ½ mile away (0825-790655).

Now you have a choice. You can go left here to Sheffield Park station, or you can go ahead by road to Horsted Keynes. They're the two ends of the Bluebell Railway.

The Bluebell Line is the most famous and one of the earliest of Britain's preserved steam lines. It reflects an age in which the occupants of country houses—according to old plays, anyway—knew the times of all trains and in which stationmasters tended gardens and kept pigeons. Trains run weekends in winter and daily in summer (082572-2370).

The route by road is to cross the A275 ("Lindfield"). Go over a **staggered junction** ("Lindfield, Haywards Heath, Horsted Keynes"), taking the **next lane right** to **Horsted Keynes.**

Don't go into Horsted Keynes village (175 miles) but turn **left** ("HK station, West Hoathly, East Grinstead") and follow signs to **EAST GRINSTEAD** (182 miles).

East Grinstead is the nearest point to Gatwick airport, which is a few miles west, between Crawley and Horley. The center is attractive, but it's difficult to leave because of a ring-road system. Look for the **A264** toward Edenbridge and Tunbridge Wells.

The **A264** takes you past a hospital and then, toward the top of a hill, to a turn to the **left** called **Sandhawes Lane** ("Edenbridge").

Follow that to **Dormansland** (186 miles). Go on to the **B2028** ("Edenbridge"). The **first lane left** comes after a dogleg at 189 miles. Turn **left** ("Haxted") to see Haxted water mill. Follow signs for Haxted, passing the white timbered mill on the left, and go into **Edenbridge** (188 miles).

Turn **right** at the **main road,** pass the wooden banner of Ye Olde Crown, and take the **lane left** to **Hever** (194 miles). Turn **left** ("Penshurst, Tonbridge, Hever Castle") and ride past the castle. You're going the same way as Anne Boleyn, less-than-lucky wife of Henry VIII, whose home this was. The village and the house and gardens are the work of the American William Waldorf. The castle and gardens are open.

Go straight ahead and take the **first lane left,** at **How Green,** signposted "Four Elms." The lane takes you, with a sharp right bend, **over the railroad** to the **junction** with the **B2027.** Turn **left** to **Four Elms** (196 miles), straight over at the **crossroads** ("Westerham") and then take the **first lane right** after ½ mile ("Chartwell").

The ride to Churchill's old home at **CHARTWELL** is uphill, but you won't regret it. The house is in beautifully rural grounds; the interior doesn't have the grandeur of a stately home, but it has warmth and intimacy. Churchill lived here for forty years from 1924 and there's a wealth of information about the man, and many American connections. The rooms are just as he left them.

The entrance is on the right at 200 miles. The house and grounds belong to the National Trust (0732-866368); it can be busy.

The nearest railway stations are Edenbridge (which you passed), Oxted (west), and Sevenoaks (through the edges of which the next section takes you).

Chartwell to Maidstone: 30 Miles

Leave **Chartwell** along the same **lane.** Turn **right** on the **B2026** into **Westerham** (201 miles). It was here, in Quebec House, that General Wolfe spent his early years. There are exhibits relating to his career and the Battle of Quebec (0959-62206).

Turn **right** on the **A25** and go through **Brasted** (202 miles) to find a lane on the **right** called **Chart Lane,** opposite the Kings Arms ("Brasted, Chart, Toys Hill"). This is another leafy climb, with a few houses set back on each side, through prosperous countryside. It's tough, but there's a pub halfway.

The straggle of houses is called **Brasted Chart,** but there's nothing much to it. Once you've cleared them (205 miles) toward the top of the hill, turn **left** ("Ide Hill, Emmetts Garden"). Emmetts Garden belongs

A little house by the sea; the Prince Regent (later George IV) ordered a discreet and unostentatious vacation home at Brighton.

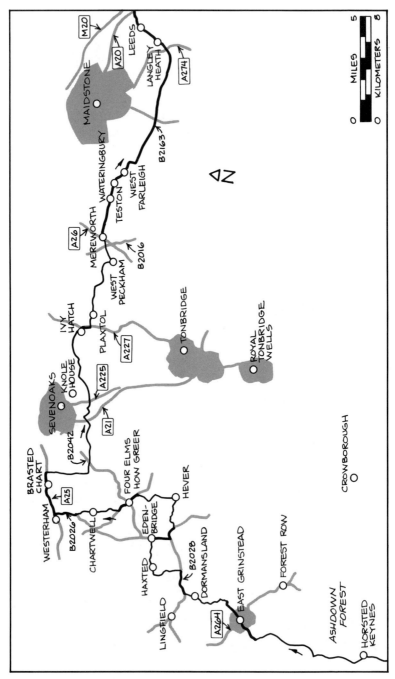

to the National Trust. Its five acres have views over the Weald of Kent (073275-367).

This is a flatter road. In fact, initially it goes downhill. But there are a succession of junctions, each yards apart, so follow carefully . . .

Go straight across at the first **junction,** crossing the Sundridge to **Ide Hill road** into a **narrow lane** with high hedges. Then go **right** (unsignposted) at a **T-junction,** go straight on at the **fork** soon afterward and go up a steep hill for ½ mile to an unsignposted **fork** (207 miles). Both roads look equally important (or unimportant). Take the **road** to the **right** and keep going 100 yards later when another lane joins you to the left.

A quarter of a mile later, cross the **B2042** (unsignposted) into another **minor lane.** This is **Goathurst Common**. At the next **crossroads,** go **left** ("Sevenoaks").

The road rolls across the grain of the land, through the trees of Goathurst Common. Follow signs for Sevenoaks, going over the **A21** by bridge, and turning **right** on the far side into **Gracious Lane** (210 miles). This takes you 1 mile later to the **A225** on the southern outskirts of **Sevenoaks.** Knole Park is now immediately northeast; the old house has 365 rooms, seven courtyards and 52 stairways, plus 1,000 acres of parkland with deer. It's open to visitors (0732-450608).

Turn **right** on the **A225** ("Hildenboro, Tonbridge"). You're not on this road for long. As it starts downhill, there's a **lane to the left.** Take this road and pick up signs to Ivy Hatch and Plaxtol. The National Trust's moated house of Ightam Mote (0732-810378) is ½ mile south. Both the inside and outside are beautiful; the interior is decorated throughout with emblems of Henry VIII and Catherine of Aragon. The house was rebuilt by Sir Richard Clement, whose job it was to look after the fat old king's personal hygiene—a rotten job, since Henry died of obesity and senility.

Ightham, 2 miles farther on, is gorgeous, with Tudor houses and shops.

The signs bring you, before Plaxtol, to the **A227.** Turn **right** and then take the **first lane left,** to **Plaxtol** (216 miles). It was here, in Fairlawne House, that Sir Harry Vane lived, the famous governor of Massachusetts.

Follow through the village toward Tonbridge, then **left** at the Rorty Crankle Inn ("Old Soar Manor"). Go down the hill through the village and look for brown National Trust signs to the Georgian mansion, Old Soar Manor.

Go past the old house and turn **right** at the **T-junction** soon afterward to **West Peckham** (219 miles), over the **B2016** 1 mile later to **Mereworth,** then straight on along the **A26** ("Maidstone") to **Wateringbury** (222 miles). Go through the village to **Teston,** ¾ mile later, and turn **right** on the **B2163** ("West Farleigh"). That takes you over the river Medway, which joins the Thames at Chatham, and into

West Farleigh. All you have to do now is follow the **B2163** round various bends and corners all the way to the edge of **LEEDS CASTLE,** where you started 230 miles earlier.

From This Ride to The Isle of Wight: 45 Miles

You can link these rides with any route you like, but this is the one I suggest. As with all the links, I've kept to quieter roads where possible, but it's inevitable that you'll have to cope with stretches of sometimes heavy traffic. You'll find it especially dense as you near Portsmouth, for example.

From **DITCHLING**, at 152 miles on the Brighton-to-Battle-and-Chartwell section, go west on the **B2116** through **Keymer** and **Hassocks,** cross the **A23** after **Hurstpierpoint** and continue along the B2116 to the **junction** with the A281. Turn **right** on the **A281** and then **left,** when the **B2116** starts again, to **Partridge Green.** Then turn **left** on the **B2135** toward **Steyning.** From Steyning, turn **right** on the **A283** to **Storrington.**

Leave Storrington on the **B2139** to **Amberley** and **Houghton,** then turn **left** on the **A284** to **ARUNDEL.** (There is in fact a delightful footpath southeast from North Stoke, which is itself southwest of Amberley; the path is narrow but only ¼ mile long. It crosses a river by a rope-and-plank bridge and continues to South Stoke. From there you can ride quiet lanes into Arundel, but be warned that the path isn't simple to find and it's more for pushing than pedaling, although it's by far the more pleasant way into Arundel.)

The effort of getting to Arundel is more than repaid by the beauty of the town and its spectacular castle.

To avoid the main coast road west from Arundel, **cross the river Arun** in the town center, then turn **left** at a **roundabout** to **Ford.** Go **west** by **lane** from there to **Yapton,** using the **B2233** from the northwest through **Barnham** to **Eastergate** and **Westergate.** Keep going on the B2233 and then go **left** by **lane** through **Aldingbourne, Oving** and **Shopwyke** to **CHICHESTER,** a coastal cathedral city known to the Romans as Noviomagus.

The **B2178** leaves from the northwest of the city to **East Ashling.** Go ahead on the **B2146** through **Funtington** to the **junction** with the **B2147,** then **left** through **Westbourne** to the **junction** with the **A27** at **Emsworth.**

Ride on the **A27** toward Portsmouth and Havant for about 1 mile, then go straight ahead at a **roundabout** on to the **B2177** through **Havant.** That avoids the A27 for as far as possible, but before long you'll have to surrender to the traffic and simply follow signs on the **A27** to **PORTSMOUTH,** which is 5 miles farther on.

In Portsmouth, follow signs for the center and from there to the Isle of Wight ferries.

TOUR NO. 2

THE ISLE OF WIGHT
Off the Hampshire Coast

Distance: 52 miles

Estimated time: 1 riding day

Terrain: Mixed; the island is generally undulating, but flat in the northwest and arduous in the south; some ridable off-road sections

Map: Ordnance Survey 196; there is also a 2^1/$_2$ in-to-the-mile Ordnance Survey Leisure Map of the island (number 29)

Rail: From London (Waterloo) to Southampton takes about 70 minutes; Portsmouth Harbour, also from Waterloo, is 1^1/$_2$ hours (there are electric trains—redundant London Underground—on the island's east coast but they don't take bikes)

I have a love-hate relationship with the Isle of Wight. I love it because it's a country in miniature, with a capital, rural and industrial areas, and a personality which makes it distinct from the mainland a few miles away. I also love it because I spent my boyhood vacations here. The countryside is in miniature, rolling in the east, flat in the north and west, hilly in the south. There are endless bed-and-breakfast places, especially around the coast, and beautiful off-road routes.

On the other hand, it irritates me because the locals have a death-wish in my direction. Many of the lanes are too narrow to ride two-abreast and, correspondingly, too narrow for passing cars. That doesn't stop drivers from passing faster than I'd wish, and if the locals have a knowledge of the lanes that makes *them* feel safe, it doesn't do the same for me.

I hope you're luckier. Certainly you won't feel the countryside has let you down. Wherever I can, I use bridleways that—with full credit to the Isle of Wight tourist people—are lovely for cycling. They're not surfaced, of course, but you don't need a mountain bike.

There are four crossings to the Isle of Wight: a ferry and a hovercraft from Portsmouth to Ryde; a ferry from Portsmouth to Fishbourne, up the road from Ryde; a ferry from Southampton to Cowes (at 55 minutes the longest but the most interesting crossing); and a ferry from Lymington to Yarmouth. Obtain details of the

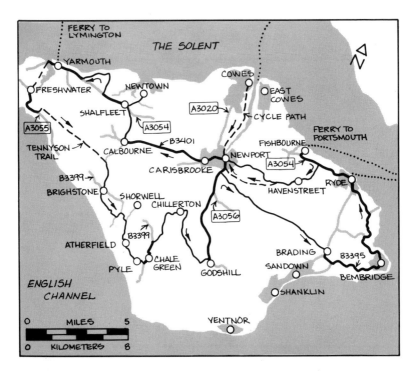

Southampton crossing from Red Funnel Line (0703-330333); details of the other ship crossings from Sealink (0705-827744); and hovercraft details (0983-65241).

I have to guess which ferry you'll take, so I'll decide on Portsmouth–Fishbourne. That's the one you'll use if you're joining this tour from the Garden of England loop. If you come to Lymington, pick up the ride halfway round; from Cowes, you can take the cycleway that runs from near the port to the center of Newport.

From **FISHBOURNE,** take the **lane** out of the port area and turn **right** up the hill to the **A3054.** Turn **left** toward Ryde. The first village you get to is **Quarr Hill,** which is really just a suburb of Ryde. You can go on into the town, but apart from fried-food restaurants and a pier that's half a mile long, there's not a lot to it.

From Quarr Hill, turn **right** on the first **lane,** to **Havenstreet** (2 miles). At the far end is a steam railroad, all that remains of steam trains that ran around the island until the 1960s. The station and several miles of track offer rides (0983-882204).

Pass the station and look immediately on the left for a track and, alongside it, a **bridleway** signposted to Downend. It's a pleasant ride, climbing gently and then more steeply. The track splits soon after the start; take the **right-hand fork.**

When you reach some farm buildings, go between them and then follow the **path** to the **right.** Go over a cattle grid, ignore the path to the left and you'll come out on a **lane** running east-west along the foot of **Arreton Down** (4 miles).

Turn **right** to a **junction** soon afterward by the Hare and Hounds pub. Go past the pub and turn **left** to **NEWPORT.** Go round the large **roundabout** and into the town center (6 miles).

Three miles north, along the not particularly attractive **A3020** and past the high-security Parkhurst jail, is **Cowes.** It's the island's commercial capital, split by the river Medina, crossed only by a chain ferry. It runs every 10 minutes and takes bikes. The east bank is where the ferry from Southampton arrives; the Royal Yacht Squadron on the west bank is where they hold the Cowes yachting week each August and a handful of sailors and hundreds of armchair admirals pack the sea front. It was from here, incidentally, that Maryland's first English settlers emigrated in 1633.

On the river is where Britain's last flying boats were built and left to rot. And on the steeper east bank are the bigger houses, attracted by the nearness of Osborne House, from where Queen Victoria ruled India and much else of the world, preferring the island to the newly built Buckingham Palace. The house and its 2,000 acres (including the Queen's life-size doll's house) are open to visitors.

There's a **cycleway** from **Newport** to **Cowes,** along the old rail route on the west bank of the Medina. The entrance is from the **roundabout** at the end of the Riverway Industrial Estate. At the Cowes end, it starts in a housing estate near Arctic Road and the chain ferry; it's best to ask for directions locally.

But it's Newport and not Cowes that's the island's capital and— since the 1960s when the Isle of Wight was divorced from neighboring Hampshire on the mainland—its county town. It wasn't always so.

The island's capital used to be what is now the Newport suburb of **Carisbrooke** (7 miles). It's signposted from the center of Newport and that's the way we go, because of its impressive castle, up on a 150-foot bank.

Getting water to that height proved a problem from the start, solved by installing a treadmill powered by a donkey, whose steady labor winds the bucket up from a well. They've got mains drainage these days, but the donkey marches on as a tourist attraction.

Visit the castle, then continue **westward** on the **B3401** through Carisbrooke old village. After a steep climb, the road holds its height before beginning to drop and bob up and down.

Stay on the B3401 but watch for a sign **left** to **Calbourne** (10 miles). It's worth a short diversion because at the far end on the right is the beautiful and quaintly named Winkle Street.

Now **retrace to the B3401** and go straight across ("Shalfleet"). Follow the **lane** for ½ mile, then turn **right** at the first **junction,** to **Five**

Houses. This is an enjoyable, quiet lane with a dogleg in it. It'll bring you to the **A3054,** where go **right** and immediately **left** to London Heath. At the **T-junction** at the end, turn **right** and then **left** to **Newtown** (13 miles).

Apart from its attractiveness, Newtown is remarkable for its peculiarities of the past and its opportunism of the present. Dotted around Britain are the old rotten boroughs, which for some rotten reason once elected members of Parliament out of all relationship with their population. Newtown had two parliamentarians right up to 1832, even though there were never more than 20 buildings.

The village survived by working salt pans and sank into torpor when the salt ran out. The National Trust now owns much of it. In recent years the village has prospered from pollution. It raises clams which were originally thrown overboard from ocean liners. They thrive off Newtown because of warm water from the oil refinery across the Solent at Fawley.

Go through Newtown, which has an eerie feel, pass the Town Hall on the left, go over a stone bridge, and then keep **right** for Shalfleet. When you get back to the **A3054,** go **right,** into **Shalfleet** itself (14 miles).

The road through the village is narrow. Halfway along, by a church on the left, is a **narrow lane.** Turn **left** there, keeping to the **left at the fork** which follows soon afterward. Turn **left** at **Ningwood** ("Wellow, Newbridge"), and then **right** on the **B3401,** following signs to **Thorley Street, Thorley** and **YARMOUTH** (17 miles).

The Yar, which runs out into the Solent here, all but cuts off the end of the island in its mere two-mile trip to the sea. The town is a small, historic port, with quaint streets and a castle, but not a lot else.

It's Yarmouth you'll come to if you take the ferry from Lymington.

From just west, the Isle of Wight is at its closest to the mainland—little more than half a mile. A long spit called Hurst Beach sticks out from Milford on Sea with, at the end of it, Hurst Castle. You can't visit the castle, and you can't get to it from the island, which is a shame. A chap called Sir Thomas Gorges built it in Queen Elizabeth I's time. It cost him a fortune because so many piles had to be sunk into the seabed. He was on the verge of financial ruin when a Spanish galleon was wrecked. The queen let Sir Thomas' wife have the hulk—something she might not have done if she'd realized it was full of silver bars. Sir Thomas was saved.

Leave Yarmouth on the **A3054.** Now follow directions carefully. Turn **right** into **Victoria Road** and continue along **Station Road.** Go through the old station and down the platform and then on in the same direction on a **bridleway** which runs along the path of the abandoned railroad to Freshwater. It also shadows the river Yar.

Turn **right** on the **only road** to cross your path, where the Yar broadens and becomes tidal, and go into **Freshwater** (19 miles) and to the **A3055.** Turn **left** to **Freshwater Bay.**

Two miles west of here are the Needles, a striking row of chalk cliffs which stick out into the ocean from the extreme west of the island. A lighthouse stands at their end. There are only three of these outcrops now, the biggest having fallen into the sea 230 years ago. The rest will follow eventually. The Needles are still attractive but the area has been ruined by tourism in general (prospering from the area's multi-colored sands) and a chair lift in particular.

From Freshwater Bay, pass the road from Freshwater which brought you into the town, go up a steep hill on the **A3055** toward Ventnor and take the **second road left,** called **Southdown Road.** Ride for 50 yards and then turn **right** ("Public bridleway, Shalcombe"). Go past a golf club, through a gate and then straight ahead on to the **Tennyson Trail.**

This is easy off-road riding—something the British call roughstuff. The joy is the superb view of the Downs and of the sea in Compton Bay. This is a route recommended by the Isle of Wight tourist people, and you'll be glad to take their advice if you don't mind moments of pushing to go with the pedaling.

Lord Tennyson, who's also connected with the Lincoln and the Wolds ride, strode (why do poets never simply walk or dawdle?) this area, giving it its name. The air, he said, was worth sixpence a pint. He lived nearby at Farringford, on the edge of Freshwater, for thirty years.

The Tennyson Trail goes up over loose gravel and then follows the ridge on the chalk which gives the area its whiteness—and hence the island's name. Go straight on **through a gate** and along a **grass track.** Ignore signs for other trails and press on until you reach the descent, which is steep. Take care. Toward the bottom, turn **right through a gate** and then **right** on the **B3399** to Brighstone (25 miles). Ride through the village and turn **right** just before the church. Take the **left** turn toward Atherfield and then follow signs to Yafford. Then pick up signs again to **Little Atherfield** (27 miles) and Atherfield Green and on to **Pyle** (29 miles).

Ride through Pyle, up a steep hill, keeping **left** at the **junctions** to head due north to pick up the B3399.

Turn **left** on the **B3399** at the Star Inn on the outskirts of **Chale Green** (30 miles) ("Shorwell, Newport"). Less than ½ mile later, the B3399 swings left to Shorwell. Go **straight** ahead into a **lane** ("Newport"), take a deep breath, and start a long, steep climb up the edge of Chillerton Down. Go on into **Chillerton** (32 miles), and through the village.

Ahead and to the left is Gatcombe (although not the one at which Princess Anne lives). We, though, go **right** to **Rookley** (33 miles) and

Osborne House: Queen Victoria preferred it to Buckingham Palace and Sandringham. (English Heritage)

the **junction** with the **A3020.** Turn **right** ("Sandown, Shanklin, Godshill").

Go into **GODSHILL** (35 miles). It's an attractive village early in the morning, before the tourists arrive and the gnomes' grottoes and cream-tea shops open. But spare a moment to look at the 14th-century church. The view from the turn, with the cottages each side, must account for miles of film a month.

Carry on through the village. A few hundred yards after the last lane to the right, on the village outskirts, the road swings left. Just on from there, on the left, is a **bridleway** signposted to Budbridge Manor.

Go **over the cattle grid** and follow the **path through two gates** to Great Budbridge Manor, which is on your left. Two paths meet by the manor; take the one to the **right,** so that you turn back in your original direction. Within yards, the path becomes hard-surfaced and, by carrying on north, you'll reach the A3056.

Go straight ahead on the **A3056** (technically a **right** turn) for ½ mile. The main road then swings sharply right toward Sandown and Arreton Manor. Instead of following it, go straight ahead into a **lane,** up a tough climb to the **Hare and Hounds pub** (38 miles) that you passed on the way from Havenstreet to Newport.

Turn **right** by the pub and follow signs to **Brading.** On the left, beyond the **second junction,** is a conical obelisk known as the Sea

Mark. There's no more to it than you can see from the road, so it's not worth puffing up to it, but it's saved countless sailors. It was built to be visible from miles out at sea, for navigators to take bearings.

The descent into **Brading** (41 miles) is steep, so take care. There's also a **junction** at the bottom. Turn **right,** cross the traffic lights, and join the **B3395** ("Bembridge, Seaview").

If you fancy a tough climb with a view at the end, take the turn to the **right,** after ³/₄ mile, over Bembridge Down to Culver Cliff. There's an obelisk on top to celebrate the first Earl of Yarborough, the first commander of the Royal Yacht Squadron at Cowes.

If you don't fancy the climb, go along the **B3395** to the outskirts of **Bembridge** (44 miles). Turn **left** off the road at a **miniroundabout** to Bembridge mill, the island's only surviving windmill. It was built around 1700 and a lot of the original machinery's still inside. It's open daily except Saturday from April to the start of November (0983-873945).

Follow the **lane** round to the right, go round the **one-way system,** keeping to the left for Ryde. The **B3395** then skirts Bembridge's pretty, natural harbor (45 miles), with marshes on your left. It'll then take you into **RYDE** (49 miles) and from there to **FISHBOURNE** along the **A3054** toward Newport and Cowes.

Alternatively, at Pondwell near Seaview, 1 mile before Ryde, you can cut west through **lanes** to Upton and the edges of Havenstreet, turning **right** there to Quarr Hill and retracing your opening miles back to **Fishbourne** (52 miles).

From This Ride to The New Forest: 12 Miles

This route connects from Yarmouth, 18 miles from the beginning of this ride, with the tour of the New Forest. The area is small enough that you can complete the circuit of the Isle of Wight and then head back the few miles to Yarmouth, rather than miss some of the best bits of the island.

Do make the whole tour of the Isle of Wight—it's better to duplicate the section between Ryde and Yarmouth, or to use another more direct route, than to leave it out.

You can use the Lymington and Southampton crossings to combine with the tour of the New Forest. The ferry crossing back from Yarmouth reaches **LYMINGTON** on the east bank of the Lymington River. You arrive alongside the railroad station. Instead of following the traffic alongside the river into town, turn **right** and follow **lanes** and signs to **South Baddesley, Norleywood, East End** and **East Boldre** to **BEAULIEU.** You can then head south again from Beaulieu to Buckler's Hard, as described in the New Forest route. The only part you miss is a poorish stretch through traffic on the leg from Hythe to Beaulieu.

TOUR NO. 3

THE NEW FOREST
South Hampshire

Distance: 41 miles
Estimated time: 1 riding day
Terrain: Gentle
Maps: Ordnance Survey 195, 196
Rail: Trains run from London (Waterloo)
and from the Midlands and south
coast to Southampton, less than 1 mile
from the ferry to Hythe

The New Forest has a place in the hearts of southern Englishmen. Of the original woods, there is little remaining. But in an overcrowded country, the Forest represents a green lung, remote from London.

This ride shows you its faces—heath where wild ponies roam, decorative rides, and forgotten villages. You'll also see Buckler's Hard, where an entire community once made sailing ships. And since the naval connection is never far, I start with a ferry ride.

This is an easy ride, with no particular hills. With a three-mile diversion from Norleywood, you can also take the ferry from Lymington to Yarmouth and take the Isle of Wight tour. Similarly, there are also ferries (Red Funnel Line) from Southampton to Cowes.

A ride on a ferry makes a trip complete, and this route begins with one. It'll get you from the industrial mass of **SOUTHAMPTON** across to the New Forest.

There's been a ferry from Southampton to **HYTHE** since Elizabeth I's time. It takes 12 minutes and runs every day except Sunday and national holidays. It takes bikes free. The service runs half-hourly from about 7:00 A.M. to 7:30 P.M., later on Saturdays (0703-843203 or 0703-333584). From Southampton, follow signs for ferries, but ask locally for directions as well because the railway station in Southampton is surrounded by a complicated ring road.

There's not much in **Hythe.** Once you've stopped looking, ride from the ferry through the shopping center. The simplest thing now is to ask directions for **Dibden Purlieu,** because the way out of Hythe is harder to explain than is worthwhile.

Dibden Purlieu is an outlying housing area, but leaving this way brings you to the bypass along **Beaulieu Road.** Cross on to the **B3054** ("Beaulieu") and you're into the heath of the New Forest.

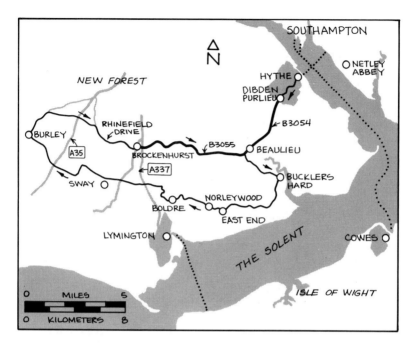

It's heathland because so many people felled the trees, which reached from Southampton to the Avon. Legend says most were felled to make room for the monarchy's hunting, or for sailing ships. Both explanations are eyewash, not least because the kings ordered more trees, not more felling. Ordinary people whopped them down, for fuel and houses for the hundreds of settlements. Nothing could stop them until a commission was set up in 1848.

Look out for the ponies that wander across the roads. Every so often they're rounded up and sold for slaughter, to keep their numbers down.

The **B3054** is the principal route into the Forest. To the left you can see the tops of the oil refinery at Fawley, alongside the river, and ahead and to the left the cliffs of the south coast near Swanage.

Ride to **Beaulieu** (2 miles) and **cross the river** by an interesting gatehouse. Beaulieu (pronounced Bewley) is the home of the National Motor Museum. It began in 1952 when Lord Montagu wanted to commemorate his father, an early champion of drivers' rights. The exhibition of old cars that he held grew into the museum. It's open all year (0590-612345).

You'd think Beaulieu would be spoiled, but it's not, and it's worth a tour.

Go **left** ("Lymington, Brockenhurst") and then **left** again soon afterward and follow signs to Buckler's Hard (still watching for cows and horses). **Buckler's Hard** (6 miles) is packed in summer. For that reason, the road is closed to cars. You can get through by bike, though, and it's worth a visit. It's one wide street of 18th-century houses.

Curiously, it began as a sugar-refining town, but it missed its mark; it was here that many of Britain's wooden sailing ships were built, including Nelson's fleet. It's still possible to imagine how these giant ships were built and then launched on the slipway that forms the village's main street. It was also here that Francis Chichester began his round-the-world yacht journeys.

Leave Buckler's Hard on the **road** signposted St. Leonards and pick up signs for Sowle. There's a lake to the right, Sowley Pond, which belongs to the estate that owns much of the area. Originally it was a fish pond for the monks of Beaulieu.

Follow the road as it swings and then fork **right** at the **junction** ("East End, East Boldre"). Go into **East End** (11 miles) and turn **left** to **Norleywood.** When you reach the **B3054** at 12 miles, cross over and follow signs to **Boldre** (15 miles). Go **over the river** and then, opposite the Red Lion, turn **right** ("Sandy Down") into **Royden Lane.** Then after ³/₄ mile, turn **left** into **Lower Sandy Down.**

Follow to the end, to the **main road,** where turn **right** and **left** almost immediately afterward ("Burley, Ringwood"). That takes you back into the Forest national park and more of the open countryside that you first saw. Follow signs to **Burley** (23 miles).

If you choose to turn off, though, there's a curiosity in Sway. In the 1870s an Indian judge built a 220-foot concrete tower to show what good stuff concrete is for building. He put a light on top to make it more cheerful, but it baffled sailors looking for Southampton and he had to take it down again. It's called Peterson's Folly.

As for Burley, the center is about all there is, and that seems filled with pensioners on coach trips most days. The road you want is at the bottom of the hill on the way in, opposite the Queen's Head. Turn **right** ("Burley church") into **Chapel Lane.**

Now the wooded Forest begins. Three or 4 miles on, you'll meet the **A35,** the Lyndhurst-to-Bournemouth road. Turn **left** ("Lyndhurst") and then after ¹/₂ mile take the **first lane right** ("Rhinefield") into the Rhinefield Ornamental Drive. It's several miles of beautiful woods and ornamental bushes which, with some more heathland to follow, brings you to **Brockenhurst** (32 miles).

The most unusual points about Brockenhurst are a 1,000-year-old yew in the churchyard and the grave of a famous snake-catcher called Brusher Mills.

Go into the village center at Brockenhurst, round a **circuit of roads,** following signs to **Beaulieu** (38 miles), from where you retrace to **HYTHE** (41 miles) to complete the ride.

From This Ride to Poole and The Purbecks: 25 Miles

There's no easy link between these two routes which won't waste some of the better parts of the New Forest circuit (such as the Rhinefield ornamental drive, for instance).

If you want to link the routes and keep in the best bits, I suggest you follow the New Forest circuit through Burley and on through the Rhinefield drive to **Brockenhurst** (32 miles). From Brockenhurst to Sandbanks is about 25 miles.

At Brockenhurst, turn **right** on the **B3055** through **Sway** and on toward Christchurch and Bournemouth. Avoid the busy main road by going into central **Christchurch** and then go south as close to the coast as you can as you go west into **Bournemouth.** One town changes to the other imperceptibly. From central Bournemouth there are signs for **Sandbanks** and the ferry to **Studland.**

The ruins of Beaulieu Abbey have stood since the 13th century. These were the cloisters. The building beyond once housed lay brothers; it's now used for banquets.

From This Ride to Salisbury, The Plain and Stonehenge: 20 Miles

The northern end of the New Forest ride comes close to Salisbury, so you can cut across to there if you prefer to skip the Poole and the Purbecks tour.

Again, Burley is the nearest point, but again it'd be a shame to miss the Rhinefield ornamental drive. You can, though, make a fairly simple circuit of **lanes** back from **Brockenhurst** to **Burley,** so that you don't have make a U-turn at the end of Rhinefield. Leave Brockenhurst (32 miles) by going southwest on the **B3055,** go under the railroad 1 mile from the town center, and then turn **right** back to **Burley.**

Go from Burley to **Burley Street** (a village, not the name of a road) and turn **left** at the end of the village so that you're going west. Take the **first lane right** to **Ringwood,** cross the A31 and follow the **lanes** which run north to **Fordingbridge,** to the east of the A338. Check on the map and you'll see that those **lanes** continue north along the east bank of the river Avon, through **Woodgreen, Hale, Downton** and **Alderbury** to **SALISBURY.**

The lanes route is more complicated and hillier than the A338, but it's only a few miles longer and far more enjoyable.

TOUR NO. 4

POOLE AND THE PURBECKS
South Dorset

Distance: 56 miles
Estimated time: 1 riding day
Terrain: Moderate with a few short, steep hills
Maps: Ordnance Survey 194, 195
Rail: Direct services from London (Waterloo) to Bournemouth and Poole

You'll enjoy this ride if you like sudden majestic and sweeping views across hills and out to sea. There are quiet lanes, a curious link with Lawrence of Arabia, and some great beaches. You'll see the odd stone globes near Swanage and the hilltop castle of Corfe, and you'll travel on an elementary ferry dragged by chains.

The best bits of Bournemouth, say the people who live in Poole, are in Poole. By that, they're trying to tell you that while their bigger neighbor has all the glitz and publicity, subtlety, beauty and charm are all along the road in Poole.

Bournemouth is worth a visit on the way, though. There are no grand sites but it's a classier seaside town than most British resorts, which are in the main tawdry and cheap. You'll find that in Bournemouth as well, of course, especially when the coach parties arrive and find themselves well catered to in midsummer. But Bournemouth's saving grace, apart from its beach and theaters, is its leafy avenues with subtle hotels and endless Victorian suburban houses with bay windows and discreet net curtains, the home of thousands of people who've come to retire here secure in the knowledge that Bournemouth has the most pleasant climate in the British Isles.

Poole lies west and inland from Bournemouth and it's certainly worth seeing. Poole and Sydney, Australia, both claim theirs is the largest natural harbor in the world. Poole's 100 miles is equaled by Sydney only at low tide. There's no doubt which is the more attractive, though. (Poole, of course!)

Poole Harbour is the birthplace of the Scout movement—Brownsea Island. It was here that Robert Baden-Powell took his experimental gang of boys in 1907. You can follow their route by ferry from Poole quay or from Sandbanks and enjoy 500 acres of heath and woods, with peacocks, deer and red squirrel (the red is almost extinct in Britain, exterminated by the gray). There's also a bathing beach, plus an open-air theater which stages a Shakespeare play each year.

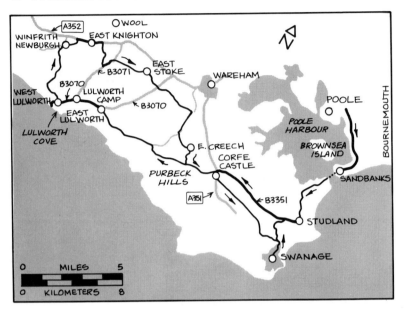

Brownsea Island is owned by the National Trust and it's open from the end of March to the end of October, although it's best to check (0202-707744).

The route starts on the road from **POOLE** to the Sandbanks-to-Studland ferry. The crossing gets busy, but if there's a line, just ride by; cyclists don't have to wait. The ferry crosses on chains. It costs 50p, lasts 5 minutes, and runs from dawn to dusk (longer in winter).

There's a superb bathing beach on the Studland side. Follow the **road** until you see **Knoll Bay car park** (6 miles) to the left and a sign for the beach. That's it. The immediate beach is clothed (albeit frequently topless in the European style), but turn **left** on reaching the sand, walk ½ mile and you reach the most popular nudist beach in the country. There can be thousands on a hot day.

Go through **Studland** ("place of wild horses" in Anglo-Saxon English) and follow signs for Corfe Castle. This is a rolling and twisting road which will get you puffing, but the rewards are the views over Poole Harbour.

Your first glimpse of **Corfe Castle** is at 12 miles. It used to defend the Purbeck Hills for the Romans but it now stands glorious, if broken-down, on a mound above the town. It's spotlighted from the east on summer nights, which gives it an eerie feel. The National Trust calls it one of the most impressive ruins in England.

There's a music-hall song with the line "I'm one of the ruins that Cromwell knocked about a bit." Since it's a Cockney song, "about" is pronounced "abaht." Cromwell knocked Corfe abaht a bit. He besieged the wife of Charles I's attorney-general there ten years after she bought the place . . . then defeated her by treachery in 1646, then took his anger out on the castle buildings.

It's open all the year, but only on weekends from November to March (0929-480921). The entrance is to the left when you reach the **T-junction.**

Turn **right** and immediately **left** ("Church Knowle, Steeple, Kimmeridge"), passing an army ranges sign. Sadly, some of the most beautiful parts of England are owned by the army, which took them during the war and returned little. Here they have 7,000 acres. In the abandoned village of Tyneham, a sign on the church door says: "Please treat the church and houses with care; we have given up our homes where we have lived for generations to help with the war to keep men free. We shall return one day and thank you for treating the village kindly." The army said they'd hand Tyneham back in 1945. They're still there.

Signs tell whether the ranges are open and which roads are closed. You can ask locally or listen to the breakfast program on BBC Radio Solent.

The **road** skirts the castle, reaches the stone, thatched cottages of **Church Knowle** at 13 miles, and runs south of the Purbecks through **Steeple** (15 miles). You're now in for splendid views over the valley and the sea.

The top of the hill comes at 16 miles. Turn **left** ("East Lulworth"), enjoy the views, but take care on the drop. There's an unsignposted **T-junction** at the bottom; turn **left** around **East Lulworth** (19 miles), and then **left** opposite the entrance to the four round towers of Lulworth castle (designed by Inigo Jones in 1608) on the **B3070** and follow signs to **Lulworth Cove.**

West Lulworth, which is where the cove is, is a pretty village of cream cottages, a little spoiled by hotels. They do mean, though, that you can get a cup of coffee in reasonable surroundings.

But Lulworth Cove *is* spoiled by tourism. Nevertheless, it's worth a look for the oyster-shaped hollow which the sea has scoured into the cliffs. It's still beautiful in the winter. A ½-mile trip west brings you to Durdle Door, where the sea foams through an archway, or stack, that it's cut through a crop of rock.

Miss the cove if you prefer, but in either case, leave West Lulworth by the **lane** directly west ("Dorchester, Weymouth"). Then follow signs to **Winfrith Newburgh** (25 miles), go through the village, and then turn **right** on the **A352** ("Wareham, Wimbourne"). As you go through **East Knighton,** look left and you'll see a spread of low, flat-roofed buildings. They're the Winfrith Heath atomic energy establishment.

Wareham, to which your road is signposted, is where T. E. Lawrence (Lawrence of Arabia) was motorcycling on the day he crashed in May 1935. Lawrence was a British military spy and general freelance guerrilla who integrated himself with the Arabs to conduct an arrogant, personal and occasionally eccentric campaign both for and against the Arabs. He's buried at Moreton, 7 miles northwest, and every anniversary a messenger arrives with a bouquet. Who sends it, nobody knows, but each year there's one fewer flower.

The cottage at Clouds Hill, Wareham, that he bought in 1925 belongs to the National Trust. It's open Wednesday–Friday and Sunday from April to the end of October, plus Sundays until dusk in winter (there's no electric lighting).

But for the moment, carry on to a **roundabout** (28 miles) and turn

Your first glimpse of Corfe Castle, from a hill a mile or so away: the jagged ruins have an almost ghostly aspect on the hill above the village.

right ("New Buildings"). These new buildings are on the map, but if they're actually there, I'm blowed if I found them. The sign is bigger than the place. Follow from there to **Coombe Keynes.**

Just before the village, turn **left** on the **B3071** at the **T-junction** (unsignposted), and then ¹/₂ mile later **right** ("Wood Street") into a wooded, **narrow, winding lane.** There's a **T-junction** after 1 mile at which you turn **right** (unsignposted) into **East Stoke** (33 miles). This is a charming road, very green, with lovely views and the true peace of southern Britain.

After East Stoke, ride for 1 mile through trees and reach the **B3070,** the Wareham-to-Lulworth road. Cross into **Holme Lane** ("Stoborough, Corfe Castle"). These heaths fill the gap between the Purbeck Hills to the south and Poole Harbour and the more productive land farther north.

There's a **T-junction** at 37 miles. Turn **right** opposite the Springfield County Hotel ("Creech, Steeple, Kimmeridge"), and then **left** 1 mile later to **East Creech** and its duck pond (39 miles).

Near here you'll see signs for Blue Pool. It's a flooded clay pit, more attractive than it sounds, surrounded by pines. The powerfully blue-green water is because of the clay.

Follow signs to **Church Knowle** and **Corfe Castle** (43 miles). This time go **right** into the town, passing the Studland turn from which you emerged previously. Now take care. Soon after you get into the town, there's a narrow road to the **left** called **Sandy Hill Lane.** It goes under a railroad bridge and then up a hill and out of the town. It's easy to miss. Be ready for cars coming the other way, because the road's narrow and cut into the surrounding land.

Keep straight ahead all the way, following signs or going straight on for **SWANAGE** (50 miles). The lane brings you out in the northern outskirts of the town, which is a vacation resort, mainly the consequence of the railroad (once abandoned, now restored by enthusiasts) in Victorian times. There are occasional trips by paddle steamer from the pier, and a regular ferry crossing to the Isle of Wight.

If you've got a few miles left in your legs, go south 1 mile to Durlston Head. At Tilly Whim Caves, you'll find the **Great Globe.** It's stone, 10 feet around and weighs 40 tons. Around it are slabs with endless if curious information. There are quotations from Shakespeare and the Old Testament. And there's the news that in scale with the globe, the sun would be 1,090 feet across and the moon just 33 inches.

Whoever put all this here has written a parting message. "Let justice be the guide to all your actions," it says. "Let prudence direct you, temperance chasten you, fortitude support you." It'll leave you good spiritual strength to refind the point at which your **lane** reached the outskirts of Swanage. From it, turn **left** and pick up signs for **STUDLAND** and the car ferry, which you'll reach at 53 miles to complete the ride.

TOUR NO. 5

SALISBURY, THE PLAIN AND STONEHENGE

South Wiltshire

> *Distance:* 41 miles
> *Estimated time:* 1 riding day
> *Terrain:* Moderate
> *Map:* Ordnance Survey 184
> *Rail:* Trains from London (Waterloo) to Salisbury take about 90 minutes

Prepare to go back into the oldest of history. Salisbury, which is an ancient city, is a mere toddler alongside the mystic and mysterious stone circle of Stonehenge.

This route shows you the stones and a few other curiosities, plus the gentle countryside to their south. It also leads you to the site of a strange gypsy curse, before bringing you back to Salisbury.

From outside **SALISBURY** station, turn **left** to the **ring road (A36),** turn **right** at the first **roundabout** and then **left** on the **A345** ("Amesbury").

After ¼ mile, turn **left** ("Stratford-sub-castle") into **Stratford Road.** This is the area of Old Sarum (to your right). Everybody's been here: Iron Age chieftains, Roman invaders, Anglo-Saxons and pillaging Danes (who knocked it all down in 1003).

It was a pretty important area, but by 1220 the authorities had had enough and they decided to build a whole new town, New Sarum, at what's now called Salisbury. But the area didn't relinquish grandeur easily. Until 1832, the ten voters of Old Sarum had two members of Parliament between them. There's not much to Old Sarum now, but you can see a model in Salisbury museum.

Carry on to **Upper Woodford** (6 miles). At the far end, at Kings Stables, is a curious clock tower with a lion and a unicorn on two sides, holding a clock, and the legend "Long live the king, 1910-1935" on the other two.

Then carry on up the valley on a restful hedged **lane** through houses of stone and thatch, through Wilsford-cum-Lake to the pretty village of **West Amesbury** (9 miles). That'll bring you to a **T-junction** beyond the village. Turn **left** and follow signs to **STONEHENGE** (12 miles).

There's been so much written about this curious collection of stones that you don't need me to tell you more. Enough to say that you get your first glimpse on the right and that you can walk round the stones (although not up to them, thanks to fencing and vandals).

Be prepared, though, that your initial feeling will be disappointment, because the stones are belittled by the sky and the vastness of Salisbury Plain. This whole area is dotted with prehistoric remains, burial chambers and the like. There's not a lot to see except mounds of earth, but you still get this feeling of antiquity.

Sadly, the army has much of it and doesn't wish to let go. In its tank grounds is the abandoned village of Imber, now all but ruined. It's sad and ghostly, with a distinguished church that's surviving remarkably well. The army opens Imber once a year and you can check when, if you want a unique experience, by writing to HQ Southern Command, Wilton, Salisbury, Wilts.

After Stonehenge, press on along the **A303,** tolerating the traffic heading for the southwest, and find refuge in **Winterbourne Stoke** (14 miles). Turn **left** on the **B3083** ("Berwick St. James, Stapleford"). The road winds in a valley before reaching the A36 at **Stapleford** (17 miles).

Turn **right** here on to the **A36** through the wider valley of the river Wylye. This isn't an enjoyable road, but it's a leg to prettier riding beyond. After 1½ miles, you'll see a sign to the left pointing to The Langfords (the twin villages of Steeple and Hanging Langford).

Steeple Langford is first and there's not much to it. Just before the church, turn **left** into **Duck Street** to **Hanging Langford,** which lies across the river. You then turn **right** opposite the parish hall to continue along the valley, shadowing the railroad to your left, to the

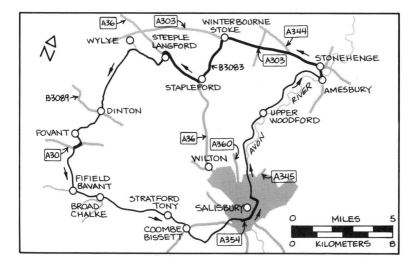

edge of **Wylye** (22 miles). It's a pretty village with some old work-houses and checker-work and flint cottages, so spare a moment to take a look.

Take the **road** to **Dinton** which you'll have passed on your left as you rode in. You now pay for your ride along the valley, because the lane crosses the tracks and soars steeply. It's a fenced road through open sheep country across the plain.

At the top, the road goes **left** and **right** in a dogleg. Each bend has an abandoned lane running from it. The first lane peters out, but the second (from the right-hand bend) is a delight. It's a Roman road through woods to Wilton. It's worth a diversion. You could go partway and turn back or into the carpet town of Wilton and then return west along the A30 and the B3089 to rejoin the original route.

Assuming you stick to the original route, you'll get to **Dinton** at 26 miles after a steep drop. Take care on greasy corners; visibility's not too good, either.

Dinton is the site of Philipps House, a superb old house built in 1816. It and three houses in the village belong to the National Trust. They're near the church, which you'll pass on the way to the **cross-roads** with the **B3089.**

Go straight over ("Fovant, RAF Chilmark"). Again you're in military country, although this time the air force has treated the area more kindly. There's not much visible except a high fence.

There is, though, evidence that the army passed this way at **Fovant** (28 miles). Soldiers during World War I cut huge regimental badges into the chalk hills and their work is still visible. You'll see them ahead and to the left when you reach the A30 by the Cross Keys Hotel.

Turn **right** on the **A30** and then **left** after ¼ mile ("Broad Chalke, Bower Chalke"). Now you're on the hillside the soldiers knew. And as with all climbs here, it's white and bleak from the chalk, with an escarpment to your left. It's hard, but there are wonderful views over the green valley to the right.

Follow signs through **Broad Chalke** (32 miles) and **Stratford Tony,** where you can **cross the river by stepping stones** (36 miles), to **Coombe Bissett** (37 miles). Go **right** on the **A354** ("Blandford"), cross the river Ebble, and then **left** back on to a **lane,** to **Homington** (39 miles).

There's another diversion here. By the church you'll see a sign that says "Village only." That's the way you want. But if you went straight on to Odstock, 1 mile later, you'd come to a village with a curious tale.

A gypsy called Joshua Scamp was buried in the churchyard there after being hanged in 1801 for stealing horses. His family, like him, claimed he was innocent. Each year they met at his grave and before long other gypsies came with them. Soon it became a highly alcoholic outing and the rector, trying to stop it, pulled up the briar rose which the gypsies had planted on the grave.

The mystery of centuries lies in the stones of Stonehenge—we'll probably never know why they're there. (English Heritage)

Upset, the gypsy queen cursed whoever locked the church door again. The headstone is still there, but the churchwardens and the village policeman aren't; they died soon after the curse. The rector then threw the key into the river to save further embarrassment.

You can turn left in Odstock, if you wish, and go straight into Salisbury that way. But the route from Homington is quieter.

Having turned off where it said "Village only," the **road** takes you down through the village, past cottages and a stream and a thatched wall. At the **T-junction** at the end, turn **left,** recross the Ebble by a hump-backed bridge and follow up the hill to the **junction** with the **A354** (40 miles).

Turn **right** on the **main road** ("Salisbury") and then **left** a few hundred yards later, immediately before the overhead cables, as the main road swings right. This is a pleasant back-route into **SALISBURY,** and if you keep going as close to straight ahead as you can, you'll reach the main road in the city center just a short distance from the cathedral (41 miles).

From This Ride to a Journey Round Cider Country: 23 Miles

The main roads in this area are direct and hard to avoid, which makes a good link difficult. The other problem is that Salisbury and Bath are at the opposite corners of their respective rides. There is a train service between the two cities, which is the best way. However, it's possible to cycle if you don't mind heavy traffic in the summer.

Instead of turning left at **Wylye (22 miles),** go straight ahead through **Stockton** and **Corton** to join the road to Warminster at **Sutton Verny.**

From **Warminster** you have a choice of the shorter but busier **A36** (17 miles) or the slightly quieter but longer **A362** (23 miles) through Frome (say *Froom*). Not much of a choice.

Salisbury: the tallest spire in Britain, and the most graceful, too. The grounds of the cathedral are a haven of peace. (Salisbury District Tourism)

TOUR NO. 6

A JOURNEY ROUND CIDER COUNTRY
Somerset

Distance: 80 miles
Estimated time: 2 riding days
Terrain: Moderate, with occasional short, stiff climbs and a long, steady climb over the Mendips
Rail: From London (Paddington) to Bath takes about 90 minutes
Maps: Ordnance Survey 172, 182, 183

Western England is farming country, with mellow villages and small towns. This ride could have started in Bristol, but it doesn't because Bristol is just another city and a regional capital. It starts instead from Bath, its smaller and more beautiful neighbor. But if you do want to see Bristol, you can make the 12-mile journey by a dedicated cycle path, which is detailed at the end of this route.

This ride takes you across the short range of Mendip Hills by the beautiful and rocky valley crossings at Burrington and Cheddar, on across polderland to the mystic center of Glastonbury, steeped in legend and early Christianity, then back by the spectacular cathedral of Wells, before returning to the gem of Bath.

It's too long to tackle in a day, but it'll divide easily into two. To keep you going, be sure to ask in a pub for a pint of rough cider, known locally as scrumpy.

Bath to Cheddar: 36 Miles

BATH is a superb Georgian spa, built on the baths that the Romans pioneered here. The most beautiful area is the center, where the Georgians built squares and crescents of light, warm stone hewn from the local hillsides. Though the planning is formal, the effect is just right. It's softened by the many open spaces.

One feature is the American Museum in Claverton Manor. There are eighteen furnished, period rooms showing American life in the 17th, 18th and 19th centuries. There are sections on the American Indians, Shakers and Pennsylvania Germans among others. Opening times vary (0225-460503).

Leave Bath by following signs for the **A36/A4** toward Bristol. Keep

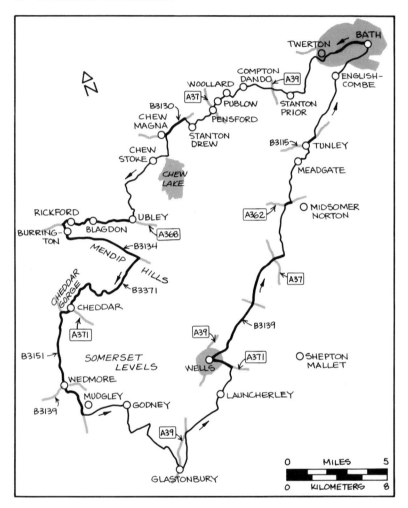

going west until you find the sign pointing left to Oldfield Park station. From that point, ignore signs for Bristol and Bath and go straight on and look for the sign to Twerton.

Go under a low bridge and follow the road uphill through shops and houses, past Twerton junior school, to a **T-junction** at 1½ miles. Turn **right** past Newton Mill Touring Centre and almost immediately **left** along a **narrow lane.** There isn't a regular signpost, but there is a private sign, "Pennsylvania Farm, bed and breakfast." And at last you're into the country.

It's a narrow lane with high hedges. Go straight over at a **cross-**

*Bath: unrivalled cleanness of line in its Georgian architecture makes it one of
Britain's gem cities.*

roads, continuing to climb. At the top you'll get a view on the right of
the distinguished buildings of Newton Park College, formally laid out.

Turn **right** ("Stanton Prior") and go down to the village of **Stanton
Prior.** Go right and then take the **second** left, which leads you to the
A39 (5 miles). Go **right** and then **left,** following the sign to Compton
Dando. This is another **narrow, wooded lane.** Be sure to follow the
left-hand road where the lanes **fork** 1 mile later.

Compton Dando comes at 7 miles. Turn **left** opposite the church
("Hunstreete, Woollard") into Court Hill. Follow that to **Woollard.**
Cross the river in Woollard and go straight ahead (unsignposted) to

Publow. Straight on to **Pensford** (11 miles), cross the road by the war memorial, and leave by the **Stanton Drew road.**

At **Stanton Drew** (13 miles), in the grounds of The Druid's Arms and behind the church, is The Cove, a prehistoric ritual site. It makes an interesting picture, with the pub for modern times, the church for the intermediate era, and the stones for ancient days.

There's also a sign for Stanton Drew stone circle, three circles of upright stones from about 1800 B.C. The biggest is 10 feet tall. The entrance, for which you pay, is through a farm.

From The Cove, go straight ahead through the village, over a narrow and ancient bridge, to the **junction** with the **B3130.** On the junction is one of the oddest little houses in Britain. It's tall and thin, painted white, thatched, with green shutters and a tall chimney with a straw pigeon or heron on the roof. It housed the taker of tolls.

Turn **left** on the **B3130** to **Chew Magna** (15 miles). As you enter, the road you want is a **left** turn at a little green ("Bishop Sutton"). But if you visit the village, you'll find the church and its lovely tower. Inside is an effigy of Sir John Hantville, who was, so it was said, superhumanly strong.

From the Bishop Sutton turn at the entrance to the village, ride ⅓ mile and then the road forks. The main part goes left but we go **right** into **Denny Lane.** It's unsignposted and it goes straight uphill. It then drops again to reach a **T-junction** on the edge of **Chew Valley Lake** (16 miles).

Turn **right** to Chew Stoke, crossing the dam, with views of the lake to the left. It supplies water for Bristol, 8 miles north.

You get to **Chew Stoke** at 17 miles. Turn **left** on the **B3114** ("Cheddar") and 50 yards later **right** into Pilgrims Way. A hundred yards farther, alongside the stream, turn **left** into **School Lane.** Be careful of a steep descent with loose gravel. It's not long but it could be difficult. At the bottom, turn **left** along a beautiful **wooded road** to **Ubley** (20 miles). It's the kind of road used by little other than tractors, but watch for more steep drops. On the way, you pass the fantastically named village of Nempnett Thrubwell.

You can now turn **right** on the **A368** to **Blagdon** or, just before Ubley, watch on the right for a **track** along the edge of Blagdon Lake. The track is far preferable, but it's easy to miss.

Either way, in Blagdon you'll need to be on the **A368.** Ride west toward Weston-super-Mare. To avoid 1 mile of busy road, I'm now taking you on a diversion.

As you leave Blagdon, with the road walled on both sides, there's an unsignposted turn downhill to the **right,** called **Bourne Lane.** Turn **left** at the **T-junction** at the end and rejoin the **main road** at **Rickford** (25 miles). Turn **right** on the **A368** ("Weston, Bristol").

The next turn **left,** a few hundred yards farther, is marked **Burrington Hearth,** "unsuitable for motors." Take that turn, go up the hill past the school, turn sharp **right** at the **T-junction,** then **left** on the **B3134** (unsignposted). Turn **left** up past a pub called The Burrington and on up the climb of **BURRINGTON COMBE.** It starts as a rocky pass and then becomes a twisting, well-surfaced climb through woods, with occasional rock faces behind the trees.

Later, you'll go down the other side of the Mendip Hills at Cheddar Gorge. Cheddar is more dramatic, but Burrington's my favorite because it's calmer and unspoiled. If you know the hymn "Rock of Ages," by the way, it was here that the prolific August Toplady wrote it in the mid-18th century. He dashed it off while sheltering from a storm and there's a plaque on the rock. There are also caves to explore.

The top comes at 28 miles. Turn **right** soon afterward at Paywell Farm ("Priddy, Charterhouse"). This is the old Mendip Forest, now long gone. It's suddenly open again, with sheep and—unusually for the south—dry-stone walls.

Three miles later, turn **right** on the **B3371** and then **right** again at the next **junction,** down the long hill into **CHEDDAR** (36 miles). The descent is Cheddar Gorge. If you ride down in the dark, it's eerie. It's also unnerving, because the crags let through and then suddenly blot out the moonlight, so that you never get your night vision. Since the rock is 500 feet high and comes to the road edge at times and the road bends constantly, it's an experience.

A sign partway tells you it's a one-in-ten grade and that cyclists are advised to walk, but you've been down worse. The bottom is a commercial mess, thanks to tourism. The attraction is two caves, Gough's and Cox's, and their stalactites and stalagmites.

Cheddar's nothing much to talk of and even cheddar cheese isn't made here now. In fact it was such a run-down place about 200 years ago that it launched a national social welfare program. There are, though, plenty of small hotels and bed-and-breakfast houses in the area, and a youth hostel in a street just off Cheddar town center. You'll see small "B and B" (bed and breakfast) signs at intervals all day, often well out into the countryside.

Cheddar to Glastonbury and Bath: 44 Miles

Look for signs to Cheddar Village and Wells (a town, not a series of holes) and pick up the **A371.** Turn **right** ("Weston") and then **left** at the war memorial ("B3151, Wedmore") and leave the town on the **B3151** ("Wedmore, Glastonbury").

After the isolated limestone of the Mendips, you're now in the flat country of the Somerset Levels. There are only three such former floodlands in Britain, the others being the less attractive Fen region up the east coast from Cambridge to the Humber, and Romney Marsh in Kent (featured in the Garden of England tour).

Wedmore comes at 40 miles. Go up the hill. When you get to the

A surprise find, and still someone's home; this is the old toll-house at Stanton Drew.

church on the right, turn **left** into **Glanville Road** (signposted, but not clearly). Then follow signs for Glastonbury until you're clear of Wedmore.

The road drops out of the town. About 2½ miles later, as soon as you're back down on the plain, ignore signposts for Mudgley, then take the **first lane** on the **left** (unsignposted). You'll know you're right because almost dead ahead after the turn is a white transmitting tower.

This is an easy ride, tougher in the wind, through wetlands.

At 45 miles, you come to a **crossroads** with the major lane running across. Turn **right** (unsignposted) and pick up signs for **Godney** (46 miles). The road swings left through the village. A mile out into the country, turn **right** ("Glastonbury") and there, on the left, is your first glimpse of Glastonbury Hill. Later, you'll ride round its base.

Get to the **B3151** (50 miles), turn **left** ("Glastonbury"), then **left** on the **A39** ("Wells, Bath, Bristol") and ride through **GLASTONBURY.** The town's interesting, with some lovely buildings, but the attraction is Glastonbury Tor.

To reach it, leave on the **A361** and follow signs for Frome (say *Froom*) and Shepton Mallett. Pass a school, go under a bridge, and then go **left** (53 miles), signposted to Wick. That's the road that'll loop Glastonbury Tor, giving you a good view on the left.

It's a center of mystic significance, a conical hill with 45-degree sides and the lonely 14th-century church tower on its summit. Legend says Joseph of Arimathea buried the chalice here that the disciples used at the Last Supper. It's somewhere below a spring which runs from the hill. At that time it would have been more remote, an island in flooded plains.

Later, the tale continues, Joseph stuck his thorn staff into the ground. It began to grow, the origin of the Glastonbury thorn tree, which flowers in winter. Still later he made Britain's first conversions to Christianity here.

As if all this weren't enough, it's said the legendary King Arthur and Queen Guinevere were buried in the monastery in the town.

When you've completed nearly a circle of the Tor, turn **right** at the **T-junction** and ride to the **A39.** Turn **right,** cross the river, and then turn **right** ("Launcherley"). This takes you across Queen's Sedge Moor to a **T-junction** at 58 miles.

Turn **left** (unsignposted) into **Launcherley** (58 miles), and then straight over at the **junction.** Half a mile later comes a turn to the **right,** unsignposted, followed by another **right** turn (also unsignposted) under a railroad bridge. They bring you into Dulcote. You get the best views of Wells cathedral from this direction.

Turn **left** on the **A371** to **WELLS** (61 miles). The town's overshadowed by its cathedral, which is worth seeing. At the north end is a clock in which knights joust on the hour. Another novelty is outside by the Bishop's Palace. Watch as swans ring a bell near the drawbridge when they're hungry.

The town is less remarkable, but the courtyard of the Crown is where William Penn preached Quakerism to 2,000 and got arrested for his troubles.

Once you've seen the town, retrace to the way you rode in and turn in front of the Fountain Inn on the **B3139.** Cross the **A37** 5 miles later, and carry on, signposted Old Down and Chilcompton. Turn **left** ("Clapton") at 68 miles. Two to 3 miles later, you reach the **A362.** Turn **right,** pass a firm called Great Mills ¼ mile later, and then a couple of hundred yards farther, turn **left** uphill into an unsignposted **road.**

You'll get to a **crossroads** and see the sign for Midsomer Norton. Now comes a section that's little more than 2 miles long, but it sounds complicated. Basically, you're riding a diagonal across three parallel lanes. But the **junctions are staggered,** repeatedly turning **left, right** and **left.**

Cross the main road into **Monger Lane,** follow it briefly and, where Monger Lane swings right, go straight ahead, slightly up the hill. It's unsignposted and unnamed.

Go under the power cables to a **T-junction;** turn **right** (unsignposted), and then, at the fork just before going under the power cables again, go **left** parallel with the cables. After a while you go under them again; turn **left** at a **T-junction,** back under the cables. Another **junction** follows 100 yards later. Turn **right** back under the cables.

At a **junction** with stop signs (73 miles), turn **left** down the hill. That'll take you past a hotel to yet another **T-junction.** Turn **right** ("Timsbury, Tunley") and pass the **Radford** sign.

Finally, after all the dodging about, go immediately **left** over a bridge and you reach **Meadgate** (74 miles). Now it's easier.

Pick up the **B3115** on the borders of Camerton and go into Meadgate itself. Go on through **Tunley** (76 miles). In **Longhouse,** just less than 1 mile later, turn left ("Priston") and then take the **first lane right** into a narrow, unsignposted lane. Go straight ahead to **Englishcombe** (78 miles) and on up the hill.

You're now back at the edge of **BATH.** Cross Whiteway Road into **Englishcombe Lane** and go straight ahead to Bath city center (79 miles).

From This Ride to The Forest of Dean: 20 Miles

The best link between these two routes is to take the **Bath-to-Bristol cycle path** (10 miles), and then from Bristol travel north to cross the Severn and on to **Chepstow** (20 miles).

The **cycle path** starts in the same part of **BATH** as the route just described. Leave along **Lower Bristol Road** as before, pass the sign for Oldfield Park station as before, and then turn **right** over the river Avon.

Turn **left** over the river and the **Avon Walkway,** on the far bank, leads you alongside and then eventually joins up with **Locksbrook Road.** The cycleway starts at the **junction** of Locksbrook Road with **Brassmill Lane,** shortly afterward.

These first 4 miles are frequently busy with cyclists commuting into Bristol. It rises gently to Fishponds, alongside the built-up area. Every so often, it runs through a cutting in which nature has been allowed to take over, so that you're in the country in the middle of a city.

The first and last 4 miles are also hard-surfaced. Halfway along is the Avon Valley Railway, a short preserved steam railroad from **Bitton** station. Soon afterward comes the site of one of the earliest zinc factories. There are still grottoes there which are mysterious vaulted chambers of clinker and mortar. It's about 500 yards from the cycle path.

The most exciting part, though, is toward the end. Just as the surface becomes paved again, the route runs through a 470-yard tunnel. It's lit from 5:00 A.M. to 8:00 P.M., but after that you ride in the dark.

Finally, at the **BRISTOL** end, the path ends just north of the city center, at the **junction** of **Trinity Street** and **St. Philips Road,** on a signposted cycle route to Bristol's main station, at Temple Meads.

The route was built between 1979 and 1986, the first major project of its sort. Part of it might eventually be affected by a light-railroad plan that would bring back trains, but the sponsors have promised to preserve the cycle path. You can get a detailed guide from the County of Avon Council, PO Box 41, Avon House North, St. James Barton, Bristol BS99 7SG.

Bristol is a city of half a million people. It is, therefore, the main regional center for western England, dominating the economy for miles around. It's an ancient town, long dependent on the sea. There are old and attractive parts, but its main appeal is for modern engineering.

Bristol's fortune grew on shipping and survived because of the railroad. It was the objective of a brilliant Victorian engineer called Isambard Kingdom Brunel, who built the Great Western Railway through Bath to Bristol and has saintly status locally. His railroad developed a name for elegance and classiness—God's Wonderful Railway, they called it—and although its 8-foot gauge was eventually abandoned for a more standard width, the romance just about survives. It's most evident in Brunel's magnificent buildings. This route is also along an old railroad route (the Midland Railway, though, not the Great Western).

Bristol has the elegant and striking Clifton suspension bridge (for which there's a small charge for cycling). More recently, it was the home of part of the Concorde project, the joint program with the French to build the world's first supersonic airliner.

The city is also the access to Wales, from the Severn Bridge, which leads to the Forest of Dean tour.

It's not so easy, though, to head north out of the city toward the Severn Bridge crossing. The best route is to take the **A4018** to the west of Filton airfield (home of the Concorde). At the **junction** with the M5, the motorway from Birmingham to the southwest, go straight on to the **B4055** to **Easter Compton** and **Pilning.** Turn right there on the **A403** to **Aust.** There, you'll find the entrance to the free cycle path across the Severn. The entrance is on the left-hand side of the approach road to the service area (gas stations etc.), immediately after the **roundabout junction** of the **A403** and the access to the M4 motorway.

On the Chepstow side, the path brings you to the **junction** of the A466 and A48. Take the **A466** to **CHEPSTOW.**

TOUR NO. 7

THE FOREST OF DEAN
Monmouthshire and Gloucestershire

Distance: 37 miles
Estimated time: 1 riding day
Terrain: Moderate
Map: Ordnance Survey 162
Rail: Chepstow is on the main line between
Gloucester and South Wales

There are supposed to be more than 20 million trees in the Forest of Dean. It doesn't have the openness of the New Forest farther southeast, but in many ways it's more attractive. That means it brings in car-borne tourists, of course, but not in oppressive numbers. It's a deeply green forest with loose sheep and crisscrossing paths.

Once this was a big coal-mining area, or at least a big area of small mines. When Britain took coal into national control after 1945, the Forest of Dean somehow escaped the net. Since then, many of the mines have closed and there's (thankfully) little evidence along this route that they were ever here. It was also foundry country; many of the weapons that the English Crusaders used to suppress Islam were made here. There are still a few professional charcoal-burners.

The people who live in the forest are called Foresters and have ancient rights, which they can exercise at an annual meeting. They also have the right, which they exercise, to graze pigs on the acorns that fall from the trees.

This is a moderate ride with a long drag to start with and a steep climb toward the end. It has an air of mystery, thanks to the density of the woods. The roads are generally broad and well surfaced and there are good opportunities to ride farther afield, such as to the spectacular valley of Symonds Yat farther north.

The ride starts in **CHEPSTOW,** which is at the western and therefore Welsh end of the Severn Bridge. The first bike tour I made in this area, when I was still at school, crossed the same river but by a tiny motor ferry. Now one of Europe's most graceful bridges takes not just a handful of travelers but thousands of drivers an hour. On the English side is Bristol, which connects by cycle path to Bath and the start of the Journey Round Cider Country tour from there.

It's quite an experience to ride to Chepstow across the bridge—there's a cycleway beside the motorway. When the Milk Race crosses, they close the motorway for fear that a pile-up on the narrow and low-

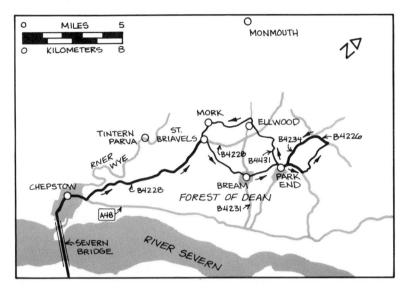

fenced cycleway would send dozens of racing cyclists plunging hundreds of feet down into the Severn.

Leave Chepstow railroad station by heading north across the Wye on the **A48** toward Lydney and Gloucester (*Gloster*). A mile out of the town you pass the race course and then a sign welcoming you to England and Gloucestershire.

After 1½ miles, turn **left** on the **B4228** to St. Briavels. This is a twisting road up through cream and white-rendered buildings, some old stone cottages, and then after a while some views to the right of the Severn estuary. Along here, when conditions are right, a tidal freak causes a wall of water several feet high to race up the river at running speed.

The climb out of Chepstow is 4 miles long, but it's not especially tough.

St. Briavels (9 miles) is worth a look. It's dominated by the castle, which is now a youth hostel. It was built in the 12th century to keep the Welsh out of England, but it couldn't have pleased the owners because they had it extensively rebuilt a century later (a century being a mere moment when it comes to stone castles). Then it took a turn for the worse before the government bought it. In 1961, enthusiasts cleared the moat, which had been a wilderness, and turned it into a garden.

Once upon a time, the castle was the administrative center for the Forest of Dean. A splendidly titled gent called The King's Constable lived here. A church on the opposite side of the road completes a pretty corner.

Quaint houses, sloping streets—that's the center of Chepstow. These are the Montague almshouses, homes for the town's poor in bygone times.

The striking face of Chepstow Castle makes a good start or end point for your day in the Forest of Dean.

After your visit, return to the **B4228,** go straight over, and follow signs to **Bream.** Turn **right** there on the **B4231** ("Lydney") and then **left** at a **roundabout** 100 yards later ("Park End, Bream village"). Bream sounds as though it ought to be attractive, but it's a disappointment. It was described once as a living museum of every form of cut-price housing that western England has tried, and that's not too wrong.

It does, though, lie on the edge of the **FOREST OF DEAN.**

Carry on to the **B4431,** still signposted to the colliery village of **Park End.** If you're interested in birdlife, the Nags Head Nature Reserve is to the left. It belongs to the Royal Society for the Protection of Birds. The road skirts Park End (14 miles).

The Dean Forest steam railway is signposted from here, by the way. It's open daily but trains run only in season, and not every day (0594-843423, days, or 0452-84625, evenings).

Carry on by the village and back into the forest. At the top of a hill, turn **left** ("Speech House, Cinderford"). Go on to the **B4226,** where turn **left** ("Coleford scenic route"). The Speech House Arboretum is also signposted this way.

The road now dives down a one-in-six grade, still in the forest, taking you to the **junction** (19 miles) with the **B4234.** Turn **left** ("Lydney") past long lakes on your left. Footpaths will take you there if you want to investigate. They're the **Cannop Ponds** and they run for nearly 1 mile alongside the road.

This takes you back to **Park End** (21 miles). There you'll meet the **B4431,** which is the road you used before. Turn **right** ("Lydney, Coleford, Park End, Bream") back round Park End, this time in the opposite direction. This time, ignore the St. Briavels turn and carry straight on along the **B4431.**

Still in the forest, the road winds for around 2 miles. Then you'll see the only **lane** to the **left.** Take that road ("Ellwood, Sling"). It brings you out of the forest, although it's still quite wooded.

You come to **Sling** (24 miles), go straight through to the **B4228,** and then turn **left** ("Clearwell, Lydney, Chepstow"). Go as far as the Orepool Inn, then turn **right** ("Wye Valley, Stowe, Bigswier"). Down the hill and then, ¼ mile later, **right** and immediately **left** at a **junction** round the side of Shophouse Farm.

The country's flatter than it was, with hedges and dinky houses, but there's still a good puff-making climb to come. Unfortunately there's also a quarry, but you don't see it for long. After it, the road drops through a steeply sided valley. Now keep your eyes open . . .

When you start getting to buildings in the village of **Mork** (although there's no sign), there's a **left** turn marked St. Briavels and Hewelsfield. That's the **lane** you want, but if you're going any speed down the hill you'll miss it.

Now you pay for that descent. The road climbs, with a hairpin bend so steep that I defy you to ride it. Through the sweat running over your eyes, you'll suddenly recognize the sturdy outline of **St. Briavels** castle again (28 miles).

All you've got to do now is turn right on the edge of the village and enjoy the long freewheel down into **CHEPSTOW** (37 miles).

From This Ride to A Trip over Long Mynd: 55 Miles

You can link up with the Long Mynd ride by joining it at Ludlow. When you get to **Park End** for the second time (21 miles), go north on the **B4234** and follow as it winds through the forest and then along the banks of the Wye to **Ross-on-Wye.** Turn **left** in the town on to the **A40,** cross the Wye to the west of Ross and you'll get to a **roundabout** where the A40 goes left toward Monmouth. Instead, go straight over on to the **A149,** ride for less than ½ mile and then turn **right** to the village of **Poolmill.** That lane then runs through **Hoarwithy** and **Little Dewchurch** to **HEREFORD.**

All the main towns you pass through are beautiful. Hereford, in particular, is striking. A character of the area is the half-timbered, black and white houses. The country is green and rolling, with small fields and grazing cows.

Leave Hereford in the general direction of the railroad station in the northeast of the city and leave town on the **A465.** Where the A465 joins the A4103 just outside the city, go straight ahead on a **minor road** and follow through **Sutton St. Nicholas** and **Bodenham Moor** to meet the A417.

Turn **left** on the **A417,** then **right** at **Saffron's Close** to **Stoke Prior** and **LEOMINSTER** (say *Lemmster*).

Take the **A49** north toward Ludlow, but turn **left** before leaving the city and ride to **LUDLOW** on the **B4361** instead of taking the main road. You can then either pick up the second section of the Long Mynd ride from here, going on to **Craven Arms,** which is the start point just before the ascent of Long Mynd itself.

TOUR NO. 8

A TRIP OVER LONG MYND
Shropshire and the Welsh Border

Distance: 42 miles
Estimated time: 1 riding day
Terrain: Moderate but with a walk up Long Mynd itself
Map: Ordnance Survey 137
Rail: Craven Arms and Ludlow are neighboring stations on the main line between Shrewsbury and Bristol

The countryside of the Welsh border is some of Britain's most beautiful. The countryside is hilly, then gentle, then rolling, but always enjoyable. The most striking point on this ride is the ridge of Long Mynd. You'll have spectacular views from the raw beauty of Long Mynd, the outstanding beauty of Ludlow—truly one of the gem towns of England—and always a peaceful countryside far removed from city life.

Go north from **CRAVEN ARMS** station toward Shrewsbury on the **A49.** Follow the road for 1 mile and then turn **left** ("Newtown, Bishops Castle, Welshpool") on the **A489.** Ignore the alternative, which is the route avoiding a bridge.

It's narrow as A-roads go. It'd pass for a B-road anywhere else. Pass the **junction** with the B4370 and then, at 5¹/₂ miles, after a descent, turn **right** on a **minor road** that starts parallel with the A489. It's signposted to Asterton.

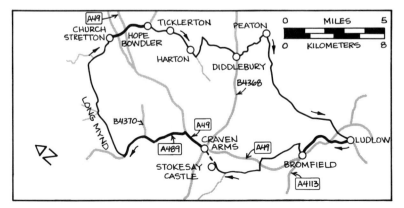

It's a narrow road through trees and hedges, climbing into sheep country. There are cattle grids to stop them from straying. It soon turns into a pleasant ride on a ridge that runs around a hill. There's an unguarded descent deep into the valley on your left and a bracken-covered one-in-one earth cliff on your right.

The views become spectacular as you gain height. You can see across to the mountains of Wales.

After gaining height, the road levels a bit and then rolls. After 8 miles you go downhill, through some farm buildings. Then there's a slight rise and, on your right, a telephone kiosk and an unsignposted road alongside it.

This is the foot of **LONG MYND,** a tough climb onto the moors that separate England from Wales. Just how tough, and how preferable it is to try it in summer or spring, you'll guess from the sign. It says "Ice: road not maintained in winter. May be blocked in snow." There's also a warning of just how steep the road is. And it is steep . . .

It clings to Long Mynd at about one-in-four. It's hard to push, let alone ride. Warning posts on the left are there to discourage you from plunging into the valley. The road climbs, turns, climbs again, above the tree line, with wonderful views.

There is traffic because of a gliding club at the summit, and there are also the inevitable motorists who include Long Mynd in their promenades. But don't be intimidated into giving much ground; you're on the unfenced side, remember.

The summit comes at 9 miles. The moors are owned by the National Trust, their highest point at nearly 1,700 feet. The steepness goes as you approach full altitude and the road ambles gently upward, narrow and through dramatic, folding, grass- and heather-covered hills. Valleys dive into the surrounding countryside, bends hiding what lies beyond. Sheep roam freely.

The surprise is that there's a golf course up here. Most of it's higher than 1,200 feet.

Ignore the turn to Ratlinghope and carry on to the highest point at 12 miles. Now you really can see the steep, grassy climbs to the left, with the sharp points and shadows of the hills and mountains. Fresh air is cheap and plentiful up here.

The descent is shallower, but things are relative: it's still one-in-five. Take care because parts are still unguarded. The sharpest descent is marked. Keep your speed down, first because of the bends, second because of loose sheep, third because of cars crawling up the other way, and fourth because of the cattle grids.

And . . . oh yes . . . because there's a **junction** at the bottom!

The junction is in **Church Stretton** (14 miles). It's a pleasant enough town, but it's known more for its literary and golf connections (that course up on the hill). The bookish link is Mary Webb, who spent her honeymoon here and subsequently renamed the place Shepwardine in her novels.

Desolation, peace and open moorland at the summit of Long Mynd, where the earth and the sky come to meet each other.

Go down to the **main road,** by the Midland and Lloyds banks. Cross between the hotel and one of the banks, pass Church Stretton station, and go straight over the **A49** into **Sandford Avenue.** Although it's not marked, this is the **B4371.**

After 1 mile, you'll see a sign for Hope Bowdler. Pass it, go down the hill, and turn **right** where the road swings left by a church, into a **lane** signposted Soudley and Ticklerton.

Follow signs to Ticklerton. Now you're on the plateau hidden by bends in the valleys that dove from Long Mynd. It's pastoral countryside with hedged lanes, farms and rendered buildings.

In **Ticklerton** (17 miles), turn **right** ("Acton Scott, Marshbrooks"), ignore the turn to Eaton and go on to a **T-junction,** where turn **left** ("Westhope"). Go through the few farm buildings and a twist in the road that together constitute **Harton,** pass the turning for Wolverton and Alcaston to the right, go up the hill through the trees, and then a few hundred yards later go sharp **left** back on yourself on an unsignposted **road.**

Go straight on at the next **junction** ("Middlehope, Diddlebury"), along a narrow road, to **Diddlebury** (22 miles). Meet the **B4368** and turn **right** for 100 yards, then **left** ("Peaton, Tugford"). Follow signs to **Peaton** (24 miles) and then for **LUDLOW.**

As you come into Ludlow (32 miles), turn **right** at a **T-junction** under the railway bridge and follow signs for the center. There aren't many places that give you such spectacular history in such a small space. If you want a cultural experience, time your arrival for the Ludlow Summer Festival and watch a Shakespeare play in the inner bailey of the castle. The castle's open to visitors at other times as well.

The best bit of town is **Broad Street,** where nearly every facade is Georgian or older. It's a good route to push your bike, admiring what you pass, as you climb from the hump-backed Ludford Bridge and up through Broad Gate, which is the only gateway left in the town walls. Quite a sight.

If you like ecclesiastical grandeur, look for St. Laurence's church. It's almost cathedral-size and taller than the castle, packed with fascinating historical bits. The most fascinating to me is the east window in the chancel. It's 30 feet high and 18 feet wide, and 27 scenes and 300 figures show the life of St. Laurence.

Once you've seen the town and its crooked pubs (structurally, that is, not commercially) work your way through to the castle. Go round the castle, which was built to keep the Welsh in Wales, and go down a steep hill to the westernmost **river bridge** (33 miles). **Cross** it, follow the **road** for 100 yards and look for a sign for the Cliffe Hotel. The main road turns left uphill and ahead you'll see a lane marked as a no-through road. That's the **lane** you take.

It's narrow with high hedges and before long you'll come across a sign saying "Private road—no unauthorized vehicles." But carry on, because you're on a bridleway and therefore a right of way for cyclists. The same applies to a gate a little later (35 miles), which will almost certainly be closed, but which has a gap for cyclists.

The path runs 1 mile farther and emerges by an old gatehouse and a towered church. It descends to the A4113, on which you turn **right** to the **A49,** which is alongside. Turn **right** on the **A49** ("Ludlow") and then almost immediately **left** ("Ludlow race course") alongside **Bromfield** village shop.

Cross the railroad at 37 miles and then immediately **left** into an unsignposted **road** alongside. You're now shadowing both the tracks and, farther left, the A49, which eventually you rejoin. Turn **left** on the **A49** ("Leominster, Ludlow"), **recross the railroad** (39 miles), turn **right** after the river bridge ("Aldon, Clangunford") and then immediately **right** again ("Aldon").

You're now on a long, steady climb on a **narrow lane.** Ignore a turn to the left at the top of the hill and pass two telephone poles. Shortly after the second pole, on the **right,** is a **mud track** signposted No Through Road (41 miles).

Take this track and it'll cross the railroad and bring you to Stokesay Castle, which is one of the oldest fortified manor houses in England, and still in good condition. The great hall opposite the castle dates from the 13th century; it's got windows far larger than folk usually dared in those days.

If you now turn **left** on the **main road,** it'll bring you back to **CRAVEN ARMS** at 42 miles, and with it the end of the ride.

From This Ride to Chester and Shrewsbury: 27 Miles

There's just one road from Craven Arms to Shrewsbury. It's the main road, unfortunately, and the distance is about 27 miles. Alternatively, a train runs between the two.

TOUR NO. 9

CHESTER AND SHREWSBURY
Shropshire and Cheshire

Distance:	83 miles; 20-mile side trip to Shrewsbury
Estimated time:	2 riding days
Terrain:	Gentle
Maps:	Ordnance Survey 117, 126
Rail:	Chester, a main-line station from London and Manchester

Chester and Shrewsbury (say *Shroze-bree*) are the finest towns along the Welsh border. The country is gentle and green with villages in which little has moved for months. The towns are magnificent, with timber-framed buildings dating to Elizabethan times and town walls and castles going back beyond the Romans.

James Boswell wrote in 1779: "Chester pleases my fancy more than any town I ever saw." Placed against North America, it's somewhat the older: Chester celebrated 1,900 years in 1979.

In summer, Chester runs ghost walks; in Shrewsbury, there are trips along the river.

Cheshire is a mixed county. You can be in the most placid and relaxing countryside in Britain and then suddenly find yourself in industrial horridness. Just as with the Cheshire Cat in *Alice in Wonderland,* the beauty disappears and all you're left with is a sickly and mocking grin.

Runcorn, Widnes, Crewe, plus neighboring towns such as Ellesmere Port, sound as though they might be interesting. Sadly, they don't live up to their names. Cheshire is trapped to the northeast by Manchester (one of my favorite cities, but not much for international-standard sight-seeing) and to the northwest by Liverpool (which offers even less).

There is a huge metropolitan sprawl north of Cheshire in which Manchester is kept from Liverpool only by some of the flattest, dullest land you'll encounter anywhere, and in which Manchester is separated from the real Northwest (the Lake District) by depressing and depressed industrial towns such as Salford, Wigan and Widnes. Beyond them is the most flamboyant and tawdry seaside resort of the lot: Blackpool.

To the east of Manchester, though, once you've escaped outlying towns such as Stockport, are the Peaks. Few roads cross them, and those that do are sometimes impressively steep, or busy, or cross dozens of contour lines merely to eventually lose interest in themselves and peter out.

I suppose you could ride this whole route in a day. But what would that prove? What would you see? I took a leisurely four days, soaking

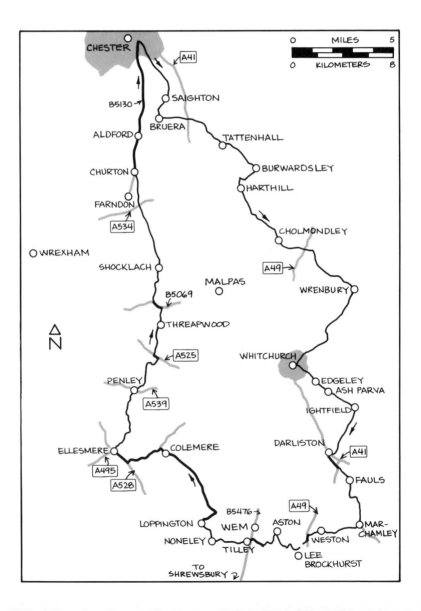

in the golden and sometimes wild country where sheep and cattle graze as they have since this land was fought for bloodily by the English and Welsh.

The most southerly point is Shrewsbury. From there, you can if you wish ride about 27 miles due south on the main road to Craven Arms, for A Trip over Long Mynd.

Because you can reach Shrewsbury from this route and also from A Trip over Long Mynd, I've left the final 10 miles to Shrewsbury as a side trip. I have, though, given details of the connecting ride in the text.

Chester to Wem: 52 Miles

CHESTER was one of three towns from which the Romans controlled England. The walls of the old city of Deva still stand and you can walk 2 miles along them round most of the inner city. Guided tours leave the town hall morning and afternoon in the summer. The streets follow the Roman plan: Eastgate Street, Watergate Street, Bridge Street (with their famous Rows—shops on two levels in the same street) and the upper end of Northgate Street.

The cathedral, the Rows and the walls dominate the city, parts of which get congested. The town crier shouts at the Cross at noon and 3:00 P.M. Tuesday-Saturday in summer.

Leave on the **Whitchurch road** and pick up signs for Farndon on the **B5130.** You leave the city with the Dee on your right. Cross the bypass by bridge, and then take the first **left** after a pub called the Rake and Pikel ("Saighton, Bruera").

Go into **Saighton** (4 miles) and turn **right** ("Bruera, Aldford") by a brick tower. Go to **Bruera** 1 mile later and turn **left** before the church toward Hatton Heath. At the **junction** with the **A41,** turn **right** ("Whitchurch") and then **left** ¼ mile later ("Tattenhall, Burwardsley, Beeston"). Follow to **Tattenhall** (9 miles). Turn **right** at the **T-junction** in the village and then **left** 100 yards later to **Burwardsley** (12 miles). To your left now is a candle-making workshop, which welcomes visitors.

Go on along a rolling, twisting **lane** to turn **left** at a **T-junction** (13 miles) to **Harthill.** Ride through the village and turn **left** immediately after it on an unsignposted fork. This takes you down to the **A534;** go straight over and follow the signs to **Cholmondley** (16 miles).

There's nothing much to the village—it's not even on the Ordnance Survey map—but it's remarkable for the Cholmondley estate, with its castle, lakes and rare animals. The castle's the home of the Marquis of Cholmondley, who with aristocratic perversity pronounces his name Ch*umley.* The castle is open from the start of April to the end of September.

The road runs on through pine forest and rhododendron bushes to the **A49.** Cross at the Cholmondley Arms and follow it to **Wrenbury**

The peace of middle England under open skies: Haughmond Hill near Shrewsbury, typical of the area. (Mike Taylor, Shrewsbury Tourism)

(22 miles), crossing the drawbridge over the Shropshire Union canal on the way.

In the village, turn **right** opposite the church ("Marbury, Whitchurch"). Ride on for 1 mile, then turn **left** under the railroad onto an unsignposted **road.** Soon you'll see a monument over the hedges to the left. It's on another estate, this time Combermere, in memory of Field Marshal Viscount Combermere, who had masses of letters after his name according to the inscription and died in 1865. It was put up twenty-five years later by his widow, who died a year before it was finished.

Turn **left** some way after the obelisk and follow signs to **WHITCHURCH** (28 miles). You don't get a good impression of the place from this direction, but the center is a mellow market town. There used to be a white church here, after which the town was named. It stood happily until July 31, 1711. Then, just after evensong, it fell down. In its replacement—St. Alkmund's—for no obvious reason, are the silken arms which once hung in the House of Commons, behind the Speaker's Chair.

From your entry in the town, turn **left** at traffic lights onto the **A41** ("Wolverhampton, Shrewsbury, Wrexham"). Then opposite the Doddington Lodge Hotel, and before the ambulance station, turn **left** at a drinking fountain into a **residential street.** The houses end after a few hundred yards and the road becomes a lane.

Go under the railroad to **Edgeley** (30 miles) and straight on at a **junction** through a wooded area, with a lake to your right in Brown Moss Nature Reserve, a pleasant place to eat sandwiches or dabble hot feet.

Turn **left** at 31 miles, signposted Ash, cross the **junction** ¹/₂ mile later and follow the **road** marked **Equine Pool.** A mile later you reach **Ash Parva,** where you turn **right** to **Ightfield** (34 miles). Take the **first lane right** (unsignposted), before the village center, and follow it to the end, bearing right at a **T-junction.** At the end, you'll meet the **A41.** Go straight over ("Prees") and then **left** almost immediately on the **A442.** Follow for 1 mile and, at a bend, go straight on to **Darliston.**

Ride through the village to the start of **Fauls.** Turn **right** after a few new houses into an unsignposted **road,** past the Old Vicarage and Church Farm. There's a **T-junction** at 40 miles; turn **left** round the side of a house called Wing Holding. Then take the **next lane right,** ¹/₃ mile later, opposite some farm buildings, into another unsignposted **lane.**

The quality of this road gets worse, but it's still surfaced. Turn **right** at the end to reach **Marchamley** (44 miles) and the **A442.** Turn **left** into the village and then **right** opposite a timber-framed building and past a sign saying "Hawkstone Hall" (now a religious settlement, with a red castle). That'll take you through the village and down a winding hill through a wood, with hedges and banks on both sides. Take care at the **junction** at the bottom and follow signs to **Weston** (44 miles).

Pass the church in Weston, then turn **left** ("Lee Brockhurst") to the **A49.** Turn **left** ("Shrewsbury") and carry on for ¹/₄ mile. Watch for a Fina gas station on your right. A hundred yards before it, on the right, is an unsignposted turn alongside a house called Woodleigh.

The **track** takes you past houses and a couple of industrial buildings. It then becomes mud-surfaced with grass down the middle. It's ridable, though. The hillside belongs to the National Trust and the path is surrounded by trees and ferns, with a stone-cut wall. It's not long, but better than the fast A49 (which you can take if you prefer).

The lane comes out in **Lee Brockhurst** at 46 miles. Don't cross the river and go down to the main road by mistake; turn **right** to Aston. Turn **left** there by a mailbox into an unsignposted **lane,** opposite a sign announcing the Spoondale Herd of British Friesians. That'll take you into **Barkers Green** (49 miles) and to the **B5063.** Go straight over to **Tilley Green** and cross the **B5476** into a **road** marked "No through road; no turning." Go into that **road,** cross the railroad and ride into **Tilley** (51 miles).

Be careful crossing the tracks; open the gate and look for trains. The first station to the right, less than 1 mile away, is **WEM** (52 miles). This must have been beautiful, but in 1667 it burned down. Eighteen years later, the remains were bought by George Jeffreys, an unpleasant character who earned the title Bloody Judge Jeffreys for his gory enthusiasm. His most glorious moment followed the Duke of Monmouth's Rebellion in the West Country in 1685. He had 74 rebels hanged, then chopped into bits to display around the country as a hint to anyone with similar ideas. If you elect not to take the 20-mile side trip to Shrewsbury, which connects with A Trip over Long Mynd, stay the night in Wem.

If you do detour to Shrewsbury, you can get there either by train or by cycling. It's also a decent spot for an overnight stop.

If you take the train, the next station to the left is **SHREWSBURY.** If, on the other hand, you prefer to ride, go south from Tilley on the **B5476** to **Harmer Hill,** south for 1 mile on the **A528,** then **right** by **lane** to **Bomere Heath** and due south by **lane** and **B5067** into **Shrewsbury** (10 miles from Wem). That's better and not much longer than the A49.

Shrewsbury's one of the best medieval towns in Britain. Look for Grope Lane and Gullet Passage, alleys where houses lean as they did in Elizabeth I's day. Then there are the timber-framed houses of Wyle Cop, and Rowley's House, bizarrely standing in the bus station. And the Lion hotel, where Dickens wrote: "I am lodged here in the strangest little room, the ceilings of which I can touch with my hands. From the windows I can look all downhill and slantwise at the crookedest black and white houses, all of many shapes except straight shapes."

Charles Darwin, of the evolution theory, was born in Shrewsbury; his house, a place called Frankwell, in The Mount, is now offices. The Severn swoops through the town, guarded by the castle, and there are boat trips. There's no shortage of accommodation at all prices.

Wem to Chester: 31 Miles

Assuming you're back in Wem, go straight ahead at **Tilley.** There are a couple of attractive timber-framed houses on your left as you leave the village.

Follow signs to **Noneley** and then to **Loppington** (54 miles). At the Dickin Arms, in front of which is the only bullring in Shropshire, turn **left** and then **right** by the post office to cross the **B4397** to **Brownheath** and the outskirts of **English Frankton.** Now follow signs along a **wooded lane** for Pikes End and Colemere.

Leave **Colemere** (59 miles) toward Colemere Country Park, due north. That'll take you past Cole Mere lake and the Shropshire Union

Shrewsbury is sheer delight—a picture in black and white and mellowed brick.
(Mike Taylor, Shrewsbury Tourism)

canal before going back uphill. Turn **left** at a **crossroads** ¼ mile later, uphill along another narrow lane toward **ELLESMERE,** which you'll reach by joining the **A495.**

The lake to the left is The Mere, a nature center as big as Ellesmere (61 miles) itself. It's one of nine which make the area a center for sailing and angling.

In the town, you'll see a **roundabout** straight ahead. Just before it, turn **right** into **Swan Hill.** That'll take you up past a church and a graveyard. The road soon becomes a lane. Turn **left** at the first **T-junction** ("Penley") and then **right** at the next (unsignposted) into **Penley.**

About halfway between the last junction and Penley (65 miles), you leave England for Wales. This isn't a Welsh-speaking area, but there are Welsh spellings: Wrecsam for Wrexham, for instance.

In the village, turn **right** on the **A539** and immediately left ("Halghton"). Follow signs for Halghton and, when you see one, for Whitchurch. That'll bring you to the **A525** (68 miles). Turn **left** ("Wrexham"), then take the first **right** 400 yards later ("Plassey"). Follow signs for Tallarn Green and, when you see one, to **Threapwood** (70 miles). You're now back in England.

At the far end of the village, turn **left** on the **B5069** back into Wales and the county of Clwyd (say *Cloo-widd*). Follow signs to the right to **Shocklach** (73 miles) and **Farndon** (76 miles). You can now follow signs back to **CHESTER,** another 7 miles on, for the end of the ride at 83 miles.

TOUR NO. 10

WENSLEYDALE
Northwest Yorkshire

Distance:	22 miles, with optional extensions to about 40 miles or 48 miles
Estimated time:	1 riding day
Terrain:	Moderate with some short, stiff climbs; several miles of off-road riding
Maps:	Ordnance Survey 98
Rail:	Settle, about 12 miles on the main route to Carlisle from Euston, London (check with British Rail about carrying your bike); some trains are direct; there are also less frequent services to Garsdale (6 miles), on the spectacular Settle-to-Carlisle line, but call British Rail first because the situation is uncertain

This is a ride through some of the most beautiful peaks and valleys of northern central England. The hills are high but not mountainous, and although there are steep climbs throughout the area, I've tried to avoid most of them. There are, though, sharp rises which could have you pushing your bike, although not normally more than a third of a mile. The other climbs are longer but shallower.

The ride comes in two parts and can be separated. The first is a circuit of the Ure valley in Wensleydale, with small, hillside fields bordered with stone walls. There are gray, weather-worn stone cottages, waterfalls and frequent villages. The second takes you into the wilds, where there's little but unfenced sheep and swooping birds. The ride is an outward excursion along the one road in the area, returning cross-country in part along a long-distance bridleway.

This is a figure-eight, really, so you have 22 miles of stimulating riding, but with the option toward the end of almost as far again of rather harder but much wilder cycling. It's easy to make up your mind once you've completed the first circuit, but don't embark on the second within three hours of sunset or if you're feeling tired; it involves several miles of off-road cycling.

The ride starts in **HAWES,** the highest market town in North Yorkshire. It's no more than a large village which has made a secondary living from tourists and walkers.

Leave by the one-way system toward Aysgarth and Leyburn, on the

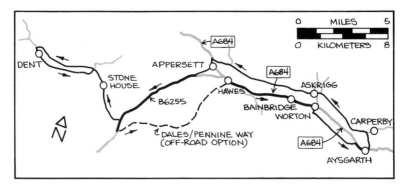

A684. You'll know you're on the right road if you pass between the Midland Bank and Laura's Cottage gift shop. On the left, at the entrance to what was a railroad station (and is now the tourist office), is a small rope-making factory which also sells tourist knickknacks. There are few craftsman rope-makers left in Britain and you're welcome to watch this one at work.

The Ure is to your left and the road is skirted by dry-stone walls. Take care to follow the **A684** on its twists through **Bainbridge,** where the Romans once had a fort. You'll go up a sharp little climb and then soon afterward, without warning, approach the village of **Worton** (4¹/₂ miles). Turn **right** to Cubeck and Thornton Rust.

This'll take you on a narrow, twisting **road** out of the valley. There are tight corners and ¹/₂ mile of climbing, but it'll get you away from the traffic on the valley road. When you rejoin the **A684,** you'll do so immediately opposite a clog-maker. Go straight on, into **Aysgarth** (9 miles).

Just as you think you've left the village, you get another chunk a few hundred yards farther. Go into the second half and turn **left** at the Palmer Flatt Hotel into a **minor road** ("Aysgarth Falls, Castle Bolton"), which immediately starts diving. Take care. It's steep—one-in-four. Pass the youth hostel on your right, then the magnificent church of St. Andrew's and its graveyard, take care on the bend and then look to the left for Aysgarth waterfall and rapids, which stretch for half a mile. The falls are shallow, but the water foams and swirls as it tumbles over slabs of flat rock. Primroses abound in season. It's worth a picture on any day.

These aren't mountains but they're still steep and hazardous, and because the weather changes so fast, there's a mountain rescue center along this road.

Carry on to the **T-junction** near **Carperby** and turn **left,** back along the other side of the valley all the way to **Askrigg** (16 miles), the traditional home of Wensleydale cheese. In a farm cottage garden

These hopeful thoughts make you realize how old some people's homes can be. This is above a doorway in Hawes.

there is—admittedly in poor condition—one of the ancient stone-and-wood cheese presses local women used before the factories took over.

There's the chance of a couple of interesting **diversions** at the Carperby junction. If you were to turn **right,** you could follow signs to Castle Bolton. Mary Queen of Scots (one of several monarchs to be beheaded) was held prisoner here from 1568. Much of the castle fell prey to the Civil War.

If instead you turned **left** and then took the **first lane right,** to High Shaw, you'll find the spectacular Hardraw Force waterfall (sometimes called Scaur as well). You can reach it through the grounds of the Green Dragon pub and, thanks to the shape of the cliffs, walk right round the waterfall. It falls 100 feet.

At 20 miles, it's possible to take a signposted turn **left** to **Hawes** and complete the circuit in 22 miles. If you're going the full distance, though, go straight on until you reach the **A684** again at **Appersett.** Turn **left,** go over **two bridges** and then immediately **right** into a **minor road,** alongside a farmyard.

You've now got a tough climb on a narrow road to the **B6255.** It's not signposted, but turn **right** and follow through the ever-wilder countryside of Widdale. The hills are unfenced, the grass sparse, the scenery dramatic. Keep going for about 4 miles, watching for loose sheep.

You now have a choice. At 28 miles, there's a road to the **right** ("Stone House, Dent"). Take it if you don't want to embark on a 15-

mile cross-country ride across the hills, and you'll have a delightful excursion of about 10 miles through the beautiful valley and stone villages of Dentdale, all on surfaced roads. Ride through **Stone House** to **Cowgill,** turn **left** over the river and continue to **Dent** (34 miles).

Dent is a beautiful village with cobbled streets. Against one of the cottages you'll find a memorial to Adam Sedgwick, who fought all the way to Parliament to stop the village of Cowgill being renamed Kirkthwaite. Cowgill, in the 19th century, was thought an undignified name. A century earlier, the women of the area turned out sweaters so fast that they were known as The Terrible Knitters of Dent.

In Dent turn back in the direction from which you've just come, and ride on the other side of the river, to return to Cowgill (38 miles), from where you retrace the route to the **B6255** (42 miles) and turn **left** back to **Hawes** (48 miles). If you decide against that diversion, but you want to take the 15-mile cross-country, partly off-road route, continue southwest (i.e., away from Hawes) on the **B6255** and go on for a little more than 1 mile. You'll then have to keep your eyes open. Look out for a bridge with stone walls on each side, then a cottage on the left, then a triangular warning sign for sheep, at the top of a hill.

Just yards farther on is an unsignposted **field path** which goes off at a hairpin, back in the direction you've come. If you get as far as Far Gearstones Farm, you've gone too far.

Take that **unsurfaced track,** cross the fence and take the bridge you can see ahead of you. After the bridge, the track is clearly visible going off across the hillside. This is the **Dales Way** and joins the **Pennine Way,** a long-distance footpath for which a celebrated walking writer, A. E. Wainwright, used to buy a pint of beer for every walker who completed it.

This section of the path is a bridleway, so you can cycle on it. It's certainly passable by mountain bike and, without luggage, by an ordinary bike with low gears. The rough section is only a couple of miles, anyway, and after that the surface hardens again. Just carry straight on, keeping to the better road wherever you have a choice, and you'll end up back in **Hawes** (40 miles). But do beware steep climbs and descents.

From This Ride to Aches in The Lakes: 77 Miles

The next ride to the west is the spectacular loop of the western Lake District, including the dramatic ascent and descent of Hard Knott Pass. But since that is the toughest climb you'll find in the whole book, you must expect the route across to Ravenglass to also be less than relaxing.

It's all ridable with low gears, except that you'll add the fearsome Wrynose Pass to Hard Knott, which follows soon afterward. That means that you'd be very unwise to tackle the two passes at the end of an already arduous day. Try to stay overnight somewhere like Ambleside or Bowness instead. And, before you set out across the two passes, read the start of the next chapter—the advice about the weather in particular.

If all this doesn't put you off, you'll be rewarded not only with spectacularly beautiful wild country but with views and towns—and dramatic and physical experiences—that wouldn't otherwise fit this book. If you've got the time, I'd recommend making the ride.

To do it, follow the route as far as **Dent**, at 34 miles on the Wensleydale ride. But instead of turning back round the other side of the Dentdale valley, go straight ahead. That takes you to **Millholme**, from where you can turn **left** to **Oxenholme** and the **B6254** into **KENDAL** (46 miles).

Go north through Kendal and leave on the **Windermere road.** When you reach the Kendal bypass, several miles out of the city, the road ahead at a large **roundabout** is the **B5284** through **Crook** to **BOWNESS** (59 miles), which is just south of Windermere town and on the banks of Windermere itself.

A ferry crosses Windermere from Bowness. On the far bank, take the **B5285** to **Hawkshead** and then the **B5286** northward toward **Ambleside** and **Clappersgate**. There you turn **left** to **Skelwith Bridge,** site of the spectacular Skelwith Force waterfall. Go south for 1 mile on the **Coniston road** and then **right** over **Wrynose Pass**. That then brings you to **Hard Knott Pass** (77 miles) on the Aches in the Lakes ride.

To make this trip, the best map for the job is the Ordnance Survey Touring Map number 3, which is one inch to a mile (slightly smaller scale than the main series) and shaded to show the grain of the land.

TOUR NO. 11

ACHES IN THE LAKES
Cumbria's Lake District

Distance: 29 miles
Estimated time: 1 riding day
Terrain: Arduous
Maps: Ordnance Survey 89, 96
Rail: Ravenglass, on the line from Barrow-in-Furness to Carlisle; not all trains stop there

This is the most spectacular ride of the lot. There are soaring coastal mountains among the clouds; sheep graze beside cold and plunging waterfalls; and there's a miniature steam railroad. If this ride doesn't make you write poetry then nothing will.

Not that you'll be the first. This is the Lake District, beloved of Wordsworth and of Beatrix Potter, who created Mrs. Tiggywinkle and Peter Rabbit during a stifling Victorian childhood in the Lakes.

Unfortunately, this romance has to be paid for. The savagery makes it essential that you stay home if the weather is bad. Certainly the ride should never be attempted if the temperature is near freezing or if fog or mist lie on the hills. If you don't discover the reason until then, you will when you get to the 1,291 feet of Hard Knott Pass. You can check the forecast by calling the Lake District weather service on 09662-5151.

The only time these routes include freak hills is when their effect is spectacular enough to add to the enjoyment. No two words describe Hard Knott better than freak and spectacular. People might just have cycled the whole way, but surely nobody has comfortably pushed a bike up it in cleated cycling shoes. The gradient, says the sign at the bottom with modesty, is "greater than one-in-three."

For these reasons, respect the weather and expect it to change suddenly; don't take a loaded bike; fit the lowest gears you've ever used; and pack soft-soled shoes for walking. The good news is that the easy bits are easy and that, should you run into trouble, there's enough car traffic to get you out of it.

This ride starts in **RAVENGLASS,** a community with one main street, a road which bypasses it, and two railroad stations. Of the two train services, one is the conventional line up the coast and the other is the Ravenglass and Eskdale Railway, known as The Ratty. Its scaled-down steam locomotives pull covered cars on a beautiful 7-mile

Well, you've been warned! Your final set of Aches in the Lakes (Bill North)

ride of 40 minutes through the hills on a track only 15 inches wide. The two stations are alongside each other.

The Romans knew Ravenglass and called it Calonoventa. The name's Celtic, though—a corruption of yr-afon-glass, which meant grey-blue river. The one street runs to the sea. Half-close your eyes and you're on the west coast of Ireland; ignore the television aerials and the few cars and you can imagine well-wrapped figures leaving tenement cottages, crouching their way down to the sea for their living. The street's the width it is because, from 1208 until the railroad killed the trade, there was a three-day market here with traders from as far as Ireland and the Isle of Man.

Low gears bring you to high places and heavenly peace in the Lake District. (Bill North)

Unfortunately the peace ends where the road ends. Once you reach the sea, or river estuaries, there's a military firing range to the left and, up to the right, the Sellafield nuclear reprocessing plant (which is keen to welcome visitors).

If you stay in Ravenglass—there's a hotel and several bed-and-breakfast houses—be careful about joining in uncertainty about nuclear power; allusions to Three Mile Island or Chernobyl won't be welcome.

Leave Ravenglass by the **only road,** reach the **A595** and turn **right** past Muncaster Castle (flour was first ground here in 1455; open to the public April to October, with great views from the terraces). Cross the river Esk after 1 mile and take the **first lane left** after the bridge.

This is a charming road, with the steep green rise of Birkby Fell to your right, dry-stone walls on each side, and the twisting Esk on the left. It's moderately gentle, with a sharp climb and descent three-quarters along. Four miles from Ravenglass it brings you to a **T-junction.** Turn **right** ("Ulpha, Broughton") and follow to **Ulpha.**

To say "follow to Ulpha" makes it sound what the British call a doddle—something easy. As you'll discover, you climb immediately. It's a well-surfaced road through bracken, sheep, and dry-stone walls. Then you're up beyond the tree line. Some bits are especially steep, although there are sudden drops. It's the top of the world.

This is Birker Fell and you won't reach the summit for 3 miles. When you do, the road drops at one-in-four with tight bends. At the bottom, you'll reach the **T-junction** at **Ulpha** (8 miles), in the Duddon valley. Turn **left** ("Seathwaite, Langdale, Wrynose").

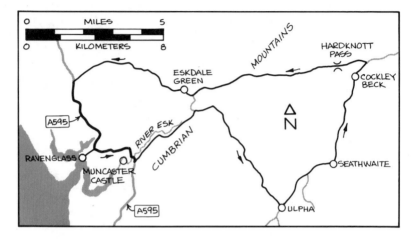

Now you climb again, although more gently, through trees and stone walls and houses. There are sheep in handkerchief-sized walled fields. The road undulates as much as it climbs.

After Seathwaite, at about 11 miles, you'll see a route to the right for Coniston. It's marked "unsuitable for motors." It's passable with a mountain bike, though. Walna Scar Road marches 1,700 feet directly up Brown Pike and then even more down the other side to Torver, which is on the edge of the five-mile ribbon of Coniston Water. The track over to Coniston is 7 or 8 very tough miles.

This trip isn't for the faint-hearted or the foolish or for poor weather. Treat it with respect, with clothes to withstand exposure and with food and lights.

Three-quarters along the way, the hill on your left is the Old Man of Coniston, 2,633 feet high. It's a draw for climbers.

The lake is beautiful, if overpopular. A steam boat called the *Gondola* runs tourists up and down; less sedately, Donald Campbell tried to break the water speed record here in 1967 and died when his boat cartwheeled in an accident that's never been explained.

Assuming you're giving this side ride a miss, pass the turn and enjoy the glades and surprise waterfalls and small lakes. That'll last until about 13 miles, when you'll run into the broad, flat-bottomed valley on the run-in to **Cockley Beck.** Enjoy this flatness and tranquility while you can, for in a moment you suffer.

The odd thing about this road is the way it aims at the front door of the very few houses. As you get there, it dodges to the side, runs round the houses, and carries on as though nothing had happened. It comes from when these roads, now surfaced, were no more than tracks link-ing the houses, so that travelers walked literally from door to door.

At 15 miles, at the end of the valley, come Cockley Beck Farm and its cattle grid. Turn **left** by the stream ("Eskdale via Hard Knott Pass"), open and reclose the gate ("Please close the gate even if you find it open").

You can now take a photo of that warning sign. You can also, in spring, photograph the lambs. There are so many, and so much bad weather, that Radio Cumbria runs a service uniting orphaned lambs with bereaved ewes.

The symbol on Ordnance Survey maps for the toughest climb is a double chevron. There are three in ¼ mile on **Hard Knott Pass,** followed by a single chevron. It's a challenge to ride them!

Near the top, where the river Duddon starts, is a stone where the counties of Cumberland, Westmoreland and Lancashire met. Things like this fascinate the British, who live in a cramped country. It fascinates them less now because in the late 1960s a politician called Peter Walker shuffled the boundaries and Westmoreland and Cumberland disappeared into anonymous Cumbria.

The ascent isn't long—not horizontally, anyway, although it gets to 1,270 feet vertically—and at 16 miles you'll start descending again.

The drop isn't as steep, but the difference is only for mathematicians and geologists. The road is unfenced and the view spectacular. In the distance, two lines snake away. The straighter is the stream—the Esk—and the other, winding as it clings to the hill, is your road. The view more than repays the climb.

Your route bucks and twists with the agony with which these hills must have been formed. The insides of the turns are one-in-one—45-degree drops if only for a yard.

That hellish descent—the steepest bit—is 1½ miles long. The treat is that 1 mile farther on you'll find, on the right, a station of the Ravenglass and Eskdale Railway. For novelty's sake, a ride down to Ravenglass is worthwhile. Not for nothing do the operators describe it as the most beautiful rail trip in Britain. The road is also attractive, but after Hard Knott, it seems an anticlimax.

The Ravenglass railroad was once a quarry line with wider tracks. It stopped running many years ago and was in ruins when bought by a company which made small steam locomotives. It runs most days of the year, although more in summer than winter (0229-717171). If preserved steam trains fascinate you, you can get a list of 130 lines and museums in Britain by writing to the Association of Railway Preservation Societies, 6 Ullswater Grove, Alresford, Hampshire SO24 9NP.

But let's assume that you're giving the train a miss . . .

Carry on along the valley to a **T-junction** (22 miles) by the King George IV inn. Turn **right** ("Holmrook, Whitehaven, Ravenglass") and follow the signs to Ravenglass (29 miles). There you'll come across the other end of the tracks and, with them, the end of your ride.

TOUR NO. 12

DUMFRIES AND THE SOLWAY FIRTH
Southern Scotland

Distance: 48 miles
Estimated time: 1 riding day
Terrain: Moderate with a few hard climbs
Map: Ordnance Survey 84
Rail: Dumfries is served by main-line trains from both Glasgow and the English west coast, although a change of train might be needed

Why, you might ask, is there only one recommended route in Scotland? The answer, simply, is to save you money. The population of Scotland is low compared to the rest of the British Isles, and the density gets lower the farther north you go.

At the same time, roads become scarcer and the country becomes grander and grander, so that in the end there is neither much traffic nor much choice about the route to take. In those circumstances, it would be unfair to get you to buy a book only to find that it takes you the one and only way.

Apart from the obvious metropolitan centers, you will love Scotland wherever you go. Those built-up areas surround Edinburgh in the southeast, Aberdeen in the central east, and especially Glasgow in the southwest. The Glasgow sprawl envelops several new towns of bleak, endless modern housing as well as areas of decline and dirtiness, particularly in parts along the river Clyde where the region has fought but failed to keep its shipbuilding and ancillary industries. The corresponding sprawl of Edinburgh isn't so oppressive because most of the satellite towns, while still there, are still separated from the city by small areas of open country.

Lowland Scotland (the areas south of and to the immediate north of Glasgow and Edinburgh) resemble parts of northern England. You'll recognize them if you tried the Magic of Lindisfarne ride first. To the north of Glasgow are the first of the famous inland lakes, or lochs, including Loch Lomond. There are areas as attractive as Lomond elsewhere, but it's Loch Lomond which has the fame because of the song. Similarly, the dark brooding waters of Loch Ness are famous for its supposed monster.

Real Scotland, though, is in the highlands and islands. There are ferry services to all the islands, usually run by Caledonian Mac-Brayne. The farther north you go, the more remote and simple, too, the lives of the islanders. You don't have to go all the way north before the nearest railroad station is not in Scotland but in Norway. The accent then becomes not so much Scottish, even less English, but tinged with the rolling and quizzical pitch of Scandinavia, from where many of these people's ancestors came.

If you venture this far, remember to take a day's food with you. Water is often safe to drink from mountain streams, provided it's running fast over stone and unpolluted farther up, but food can be a problem. So, too, can midges and other biting insects in summer and fall.

Lastly, don't underestimate the scale of Scotland. It looks pretty small alongside Texas, but it's more than a weekend's ride to see.

This is a ride that takes you round one of the most placid and poetic coasts in Europe, past a beautiful abbey appropriately called Sweetheart, and then back over wilder country to where you started. Come and enjoy the beauty and the solitude of the Solway coast—and enjoy its connections with one of the first American heroes and with Scotland's greatest poet.

Robert Burns is to Scotland what William Shakespeare is to England. As many parts of Scotland as can contrive to lay claim to him

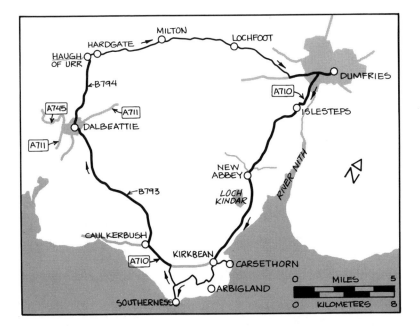

Robert Burns is to Scottish literature what William Shakespeare is to the English. This is his house in Dumfries. (Roddy Simpson, Dumfries and Galloway Tourist Board)

do so with enthusiasm. Dumfries (say **Dum-freece**) leads them all, but without contriving.

Burns had a farm at Ellisland, six miles northeast on the Kilmarnock road. Dumfries made him a tax collector and he moved into the town in 1791, first in Bank Street and then in Mill Vennel, which is now called Burns Street.

In Burns Street is Burns House, a small house and museum which has the chair in which he wrote his last poems plus other relics. It's open daily in summer and Tuesday–Saturday in winter (0387-55297). Burns is buried in the graveyard of St. Michael's church, close by.

The name Dumfries comes from Dun or Drum Pheas, which means the fort or ridge in the brushwood. Among its visitors was Bonnie Prince Charlie, who tried to rally support for the Jacobites. When he saw the town wasn't keen, he took $6,000 from them and also 1,000 pairs of shoes, for his soldiers.

Leave **DUMFRIES** by going through the town westward. Pick up signs for "Solway Coast, A710."

Ride through to the edge of Dumfries (2 miles) and carry on along the **A710.** Despite being a main road, it's quite enjoyable, which is just as well because there's no alternative. It's generally a feature of Scotland (although highland rather than lowland Scotland) that roads are quieter than their equivalent in southern England.

This road has just one lane in each direction. It goes through rich, pastoral dairy country with bright green hills to all sides. There are far views of valleys with trees and hedges and small woods, with animals grazing on the bottoms of round-topped mountains.

Go on through **Islesteps** (4 miles). Soon after that you'll see signs for Shambellie House, which is a costume museum. And then you'll get to **New Abbey** (8 miles). With whitewashed cottages, a water mill and an old smithy, it'd be a beautiful village in its own right. But at one end is the beautifully named Sweetheart Abbey, which is on your left. It's owned by the state and it's open all year during the day. It's an old building, seemingly of warm, red brick, not of stone like other castles. The roof has gone. Above the door of the smithy is the reminder that

> *By Hammer and Hand*
> *All Arts do Stand.*

A mile away, above Glen Burn, is the Waterloo Tower "To our Gallant Prussian Allies under Marshal Blücher."

Carry on along the road from New Abbey, still skirting the mountains to your right. It's clear how far the tree level goes. And then, ahead, you'll suddenly see the broad, glistening expanse of Solway Firth, the water reaching across to England on the far bank.

Ride on to **Kirkbean** (say *K'been*) (13 miles). This was the birthplace of George Washington's friend, Dr. James Craik, who set up the American Army's medical service.

Turn **left** in the village ("Carsethorne") and ride down into **Carsethorne** village. The road turns **right** at the start of the village (15 miles) and then runs along the edge of the Solway for about $\frac{1}{2}$ mile before fizzling out just before the water's edge.

There's not a lot here, although there is a shop and a pub (one of the few places to have a meal or a drink on the whole of this ride, by the way; the rural sections are frequently sparsely populated). But it is a pleasant place to sit and idle away a few moments, walking along the stony beach and staring at the fishing boats and the water, or strolling alongside the brilliantly white-painted cottages.

One day the whole village will be here no longer, because little by little it's disappearing into the sea. But while it lasts, the residents seem to have made a point of taking a real pride in it.

There's not much for them to do these days, but Carsethorne was a schooner port in the 1920s. In 1850 alone, it sent 10,000 emigrants to Canada and 11,000 to Australia and New Zealand. The coast guard house at the far end of the village suggests that the inbound traffic wasn't always as honest.

Your exploration over, retrace by the **only road** but don't go as far as the main road. Instead, just before it, turn **left** ("Arbigland"). It's level at first but then climbs through small woods to a **T-junction** at the top of the hill.

Right ahead of you **Arbigland Garden** is signposted to the left. It's open on Tuesdays, Thursdays and Sundays in the afternoon from May to September. It was here that John Paul "I have not yet begun to fight" Jones was born, in 1747. He had the effrontery to be the first person in four centuries to attack Britain from the sea, taking it into his head to sail up and down the coast popping off at whatever he could get in his gunsights. It was all part of obeying orders to "distress the enemies of the United States." The damage wasn't often great, but it caused great offense (more details of this in the Magic of Lindisfarne ride, incidentally).

Jones' father was gardener to merchants in Dumfries who eventually left him a slab of Virginia. Jones, who'd been at sea off and on since he was 12, moved to America and turned against his homeland in the War of Independence. His ship is said to have been the first to have flown the Stars and Stripes.

There's a memorial to him in the church at Kirkbean, put there by wartime American sailors, "the officers and men of the US Navy who served in Great Britain under the command of Admiral Harold R. Stark."

Turn **right** at the entrance to the garden (unsignposted), following the **road.** Catch glimpses to the right of the Solway Firth again. The mountain also to your right is called Criffel. It's 1,868 feet high, the highest of the little batch of hills southeast of Dumfries. You can climb to the top if you wish to verify claims that Ireland and the Isle of Man are visible from the summit. The twin peak is called Knockendoch.

When you get to another **T-junction** (18 miles), turn **left** ("Southerness") to **Southerness** (22 miles). This is something of a disappointment after Kirkbean because it's commercialized, which is not an adjective you'd apply to Kirkbean. There is, though, a chance of a drink and something to eat and your last good views of the sea.

Turn round at the end of the road, amid the vacation homes and shops, and **retrace.** Now take the **first lane left** (unsignposted), which you can identify because 50 yards along it is a sign reading "Passing place."

Pass the tower of a ruined church, follow the road to the **right,** and ride on to a **T-junction.** Turn **left** back on the **main road** to **Mainsriddle** (24 miles).

Go over an old bridge on the outskirts of **Caulkerbush** and turn **right** on the **B793** ("Dalbeattie"). This is a lovely lane with woods, open farmland and stone walls, with some fine views. It climbs gently and, as you get higher, the country changes as the land becomes less fertile and rockier. You move from arable into sheep country, until finally above the grassline (the fields are now of rock and heather), you start going back downhill again.

The descent is more wooded than the rise, with views of surrounding hills. And then you come to **DALBEATTIE** (33 miles). It's a gray,

The warm grace of Sweetheart Abbey—surely the most beautiful name of any church building in Britain? (Roddy Simpson, Dumfries and Galloway Tourist Board)

forbidding town as so many Scottish towns are when the main building material is granite. The buildings are made of square-cut stone,
which does nothing to make them warmer.

Granite quarrying made the town's fortune and it's Dalbeattie granite which lines the Thames embankment in London as well as many
other important sites around the world. Sadly, somehow, the quarry
now produces only granite chippings for road surfacing.

Turn **right** at the **T-junction** and go through the center of town,
over the bridge, past the tourist information office. Then turn **left**
("A711, Castle Douglas"). Follow the road and then turn **right** by a
church onto the **B794** ("Hough of Urr"). Now you're on another steady
climb, again rewarded by views. This is green and open country, very
pleasing and stimulating, the hills all around you.

Haugh of Urr comes at **38 miles.** Turn **right** ("Hardgate, Milton")
just after the post office into **School Brae.** Go up the hill past some
white and colored bungalows. That takes you out of the village
through more open country and almost immediately into **Hardgate**
(39 miles).

The road now rolls but goes mainly downhill through more green
fields and stone walls. The country is now getting harder for cycling,
with some puff-making climbs as we head back across the hills to the
few houses of **Milton** (42 miles) and **Lochfoot** (46 miles) (which at
least has a pub) to the **main road** (47 miles) to **DUMFRIES** (48
miles).

TOUR NO. 13

THE MAGIC OF LINDISFARNE
The Northumberland Coast

Distance: 80 miles
Estimated time: 2 riding days
Terrain: Moderate with a few hard climbs
Maps: Ordnance Survey 74, 75, 81
Rail: Alnmouth is on the line from Newcastle upon Tyne to Berwick-upon-Tweed

Nobody knows who wrote these lines, but they sum up the area well:

Hills bathed in purple distance stand
Like giants 'neath some fairy spell.
A thousand birds sing clear and tell
'Tis summer time on Borderland!

This ride lives up to that well. You'll sweep along the glorious Northumberland coast with its calling birds and its broad, unspoiled sands. You'll find breathtaking castles. And you'll go back to early history with the unique ride across the sea to Holy Island and the remote mysticism of Lindisfarne.

Then comes the solitude of the hills below the Cheviot mountains, followed by the beauty of the castle town of Alnwick.

This whole area—like the border between England and Wales—has been fought over repeatedly by the neighboring nations. It happened as long ago as Roman times. The Romans saw Scotland starting south of where we've now put it and built a wall 73 miles long from the Solway Firth to Newcastle upon Tyne to keep the Scots in place.

The Emperor Hadrian gave his order in A.D. 122 and work started immediately. The Romans built it up to 20 feet high and 9 feet wide and studded it with forts, turrets and signal towers. A ditch made the wall still more difficult to scale.

A lot of the wall is still there and it's worth a look. The western and central sections are generally better than the eastern end, not least because the eastern bit lies now in the suburbs of Newcastle. The other parts are largely in the country. Best of all is the section between Sewingshields and Gilsland. These 15 miles or so include the old Housteads infantry fort, which housed 1,000 men.

The wall is breached rather than followed by roads, but the B6318

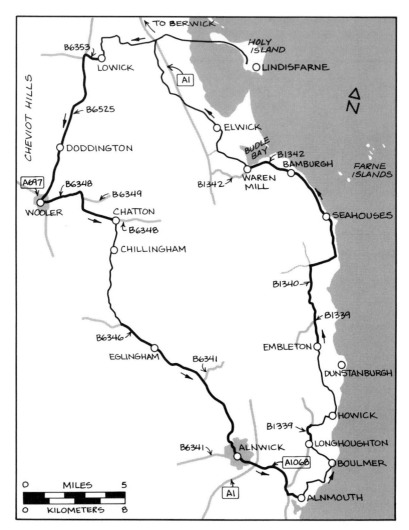

east of Haltwhistle (some way east of Carlisle and a third of the way along the wall), runs within striking distance of the best bits.

If you call English Heritage in London (071-973 3457) and ask for the pamphlet "Hadrian's Wall: Exploring Roman Northumberland," you'll get a simple map and a description of the remaining sections of wall. You can also get details from the tourist office at the Manor House, Hallgate, Hexham NE46 1XD (0434-605225).

Alnwick to Lindisfarne: 40 Miles

This rides starts just outside **ALNWICK** (say *Annick*), in the seaside village of **Alnmouth.** It used to ship a lot of grain but now it's simply a small and attractive summer vacation spot, with pleasing houses and a coastal golf course.

Two bizarre events stud its history. In 1779, the American John Paul Jones was cruising the coast in his role of aggravating the British (for more about Jones, see the Dumfries and the Solway Firth ride). Spotting the village church, he fired a gun at it. He missed. Instead, the 68-pound cannonball bounced three times along the ground and hit the end of a farmhouse, doing it no good at all.

People were still talking about this curious event when, in 1806, there was a great gale and the sea broke through, flooded part of the town and moved the course of the river Aln. When it moved, unfortunately, it also left the harbor stranded and the grain ships could no longer call. Alnmouth was never the same again.

Leave the village by the **roundabout** on the outskirts. Take the **exit** signposted "Foxton, Boulmer." You leave with the river winding to your left and immediately start going uphill. The countryside already looks more like the Scottish lowlands than southern England, with mossy grass, open fields and stone walls. To the right are glimpses of the sea, with beautiful sandy beaches (if only the beaches were justified by the climate, they'd be the most wonderful in Europe).

At the first **T-junction** (1 mile) turn **right** (unsignposted) toward Boulmer. The **lane** takes you round the edge of a golf course and directly toward the sea, and into **Boulmer** (3 miles).

There's a lifeboat station, a pub, stone houses and not much else. Follow the road through the village—there's not much choice—as it swings back inland toward Longhoughton.

This Northumberland coast can (as Alnmouth will testify) be battered by winter storms, which explains the sparseness of the fields and the stubborn stoneness of the buildings, as well as the resigned look of animals in the fields. The houses are built low, to keep them down out of the easterly wind and the sea spray.

Go past the RAF camp, which is extensive and has a disused jet aircraft marking the entrance. After the RAF station, you reach the **B1339** (5 miles). Turn **right** ("Craster, Seahouses") into the village of **Longhoughton.**

Follow signs to Howick, which means leaving the B-road by going straight on at a bend. The **road** to Craster (a town famed for its kippers—smoked herrings) goes through pleasant woods, past the entrance to Howick Hall Gardens, a collection of extensive grounds and shrubs in a woodland garden around the building of Howick Hall. It's open in the afternoon from April to September (0665-577285).

Howick (7 miles) is a tiny but more striking coastal village, with older stone houses, mellowed in color. Not much more to it than that, though. At the **T-junction** within sight of the sea, turn **left** ("Craster"). This is a charming road which rolls gently. It's clear that rock lies under the surface earth, with stone walls on both sides, a moorland look with crags of stone covered in clumps of olive-green grass. This is sheep country and you're likely to be stopped by flocks being herded along the road.

Craster lies to the right along this road and you'll see signs for there and for Dunstanburgh Castle, 2 miles away.

DunstanburghCastle is one of Britain's most atmospheric. It stands 100 feet above the sea on a crag of basalt. You'd think that'd make it invincible, and presumably that's what the Earl of Lancaster thought when he built it. But it suffered a great deal during the War of the Roses and not a lot remains apart from the gatehouse and the curtain wall. What's left, though, is interesting for its shape and for the birdlife that thrives around it.

It was the home of John of Gaunt and became a royal castle when John's son, Bolingbroke, became Henry IV. It belongs to English Heritage and it's open daily between Easter and the end of September and from Tuesday–Sunday the rest of the year.

After your visit, return to the **junction** and go straight on ("Embleton, Newton, Seahouses"). Even if you choose not to visit the castle, you'll still get a good view of its crags and towers, to the right 1 mile later.

Embleton comes at 12 miles. Go through the village and meet the **B1339** opposite the church. Turn **right** ("Beadnell, Seahouses") and follow the **B1340** round the outside of **Beadnell** (17 miles), into **Seahouses** (19 miles).

Two to five miles off the coast near Seahouses are the thirty Farne islands, which are home during the summer for eighteen species of seabirds. There are great numbers of puffins, and also cormorants, eiders, razorbills, oystercatchers, ringed plovers and guillemots. There's also a large colony of gray seals. You can visit at different times of the year (late May and early June are best for bird-watching) but access is limited. Check with the National Trust (0665-721099). It'll also give you the numbers of ferrymen who'll take you out from the mainland.

In Seahouses, turn **right** at a little **roundabout,** still on the **B1340** ("Bamburgh"). That takes you through the middle of town, which is very much a vacation spot, with lots of shops selling lettered rock (long sticky pink tubes of candy, with lettering printed internally along its length) and beach items.

Straight ahead as you go along the coast, you see **Bamburgh Castle,** a substantial place to say the least. It's a striking building on a rise overlooking the sea 150 sheer feet below it, and you see it from miles back, its tall, narrow and seemingly windowless walls looking impregnable. As you get close, the castle disappears for a moment behind some trees on a mound on the right. And then suddenly it jumps out at you with great drama. It marks the days when Northumbria was a kingdom and Bamburgh its capital.

When royalty moved out, the building was used variously as a surgery and dispensary for the poor, a training school for servant girls, a windmill to grind poor people's corn, and a haven for shipwrecked sailors. Finally, Lord Armstrong restored it ninety years ago and it's now open in the afternoon from April to the end of October (06684-208).

Bamburgh village (22 miles) was the site of a dramatic sea rescue. It happened on September 7, 1838, when a man called William Darling was the keeper of the Longstone lighthouse, in the Farne islands. That day the steamer *Forfarshire* was wrecked on the islands. With the gale still at its peak, Darling and his 23-year-old daughter, Grace, set out in a fragile 21-foot rowing boat. They rescued four men and a woman.

Two of the men joined Darling on another expedition and saved four more. Sadly, Grace Darling died shortly afterward and she's buried now in the village graveyard, where there's an elaborate memorial to her. The boat in which she and her father made themselves heroes is in the village museum, open from late March to the end of September. It's opposite the church.

Go straight through ("Berwick") on the **B1342**. Go round the end of Budle Bay into **Waren Mill** (25 miles). There's not much to the village, but at the far end the B1342 goes off to the left and you go **straight on** ("Holy Island, Berwick"). You say *Berrick,* by the way.

The country is more prosperous-looking—nothing like southern England, but there are more crops now and the grass is greener.

Ignore signs for Holy Island, even though that's where we're going, and head instead for Elwick. The point of coming this way is that it avoids most of the A1 and ignores the way most of the tourist traffic goes, while itself not being much out of the way.

Elwick (29 miles) isn't much and the lane runs out over the railroad to the main road, the **A1** (31 miles). For most of the way, the A1 (the main highway from London to Newcastle and Edinburgh) is virtually and sometimes actually a motorway. Here, though, there's just one lane in each direction.

Turn **right** on the A1 and then ½ mile later turn **left** ("Buckton"). This is another detour to avoid the A1. The hills ahead are the Kyloes, not notable in themselves except that they mark the start of the Cheviot mountain range, which makes the backbone of northern England. You can also see the start of some dark green woods. Plantations of this sort are more Scottish than English and they're also controversial. For some years the government gave tax incentives for planting trees, but critics say the result is that great sweeps of conifers now cover hillsides where they're not native. This forestation is more apparent in the highlands of Scotland.

At 32 miles, you reach a **T-junction.** Turn **right** (unsignposted) into **Fenwick** (33 miles) and to a junction, at which you turn **left** (unsignposted) to leave the village again. Don't ride too far; just after Fenwick school, which is now a bed-and-breakfast place, take the fork to the **right** (unsignposted). That climbs attractively up a ridge, the road just wide enough for a couple of bike riders. It doesn't go anywhere in particular except that it brings you back on to the **A1** (35 miles).

Turn **left** and immediately ahead you'll see signs for Beale and Holy Island. Turn **right** into that **lane** at the far end of the Plough hotel. On the **junction,** once you've turned right, you'll see tide tables displayed. It's important that you consult them because the road to Holy Island is ridable only at low tide. It's a causeway and the tide rises fast. Don't be tempted to make the crossing at the last moment because it's a ride of 3 miles and you will, without doubt, be submerged.

Those tide tables are pinned up again just before you reach the causeway across to the island. The crossing is marked by poles and is well surfaced. It's an appealing road, only just higher than the water even at low tide. It gives you an eerie feeling, particularly when you look to either side at the expanse of sea that you're crossing. The island, which looks dull from a distance, now starts to look more interesting.

There will be other traffic on this road, so even if it's not in your character, now's the time to be assertive. The only choices are to ride on the road or in the water; if you're not happy about drivers overtaking you, keep far out enough into the road to control whether it happens or not. You'll find most people friendly and understanding, and the chances are that you'll cross in perfect safety . . . but to be brushed or startled into the water isn't fun.

High sandy dunes eventually replace the sea. The dunes are fenced off because the area's a nature reserve. **HOLY ISLAND** and Lindisfarne come at 40 miles.

Check the tide tables again because your time on the island is governed by the sea, of course. The longest you're likely to be "trapped" (a not unpleasant experience, incidentally) is 4 hours. You can stay the night in one of several bed-and-breakfast houses, but since tourism is busy and the number of beds is obviously limited, it's best to call the tourist information office first and ask for phone numbers.

Holy Island is well named. Lindisfarne—the name means island of the Lindsey travelers—is one of Christianity's most important early centers. But don't think that it's just a living museum; the village is a thriving one of 250 people—albeit a smaller population than in years

Castle catering: how things used to be in the kitchen of Lindisfarne Castle.
(British Insulated Callender's Cables)

gone by and also cut off from the mainland for several hours twice a day. They pass their days fishing, or looking after tourists, or making honey and liqueur.

Lindisfarne Priory's best seen against the evening sun, when the curve of the decorated rainbow arch looks wonderful against the evening reds and yellows. The priory's open daily from Easter or April 1, whichever comes first, to the end of September. It's open Tuesday–Sunday at other times. It belongs to English Heritage (0289-89200).

The dramatic castle on its great isolated mound overlooking the harbor belongs to the National Trust. It's open on different days during the year (0289-89244).

Off the coast near the priory is St. Cuthbert's Island. St. Cuthbert is the island's ancient saint, and if you can cross the few hundred yards out to the island, you can stand by the stone cross on the site of the Saxon chapel. It was here that he came for seclusion. St. Cuthbert had a softer spot for the Farne islands than he did for Lindisfarne, and it was only when he was dying that he decided to be buried at Lindisfarne instead.

The other saint was Aidan, a Celt who founded the monastery in 635 after getting the island from Oswald, the king of Northumbria, who wanted him to convert the pagans. The Danes came trampling in, though, and the monks ran for their lives, taking St. Cuthbert's body with them (it's now in Durham cathedral). Upset, the Danes came back and pulled down the monastery.

Lindisfarne to Alnmouth: 40 Miles

To return from the island, take the causeway that you used on the route in. That brings you back to the A1. If you wish, you can now make an 8-mile excursion right to Berwick-upon-Tweed, the most northerly town in England.

Berwick is a highly picturesque town of gray or reddish-brown stone. It looks as though a giant picked up all the houses and sprinkled them on a rocky peninsula. There are some handsome buildings and a faint air of frontier town—which is just what it is, of course. Although it's in England, tradition holds that it's in neither England nor Scotland. That's because the border moved north or south of the town about 20 times before, in 1482, it finally settled to the north.

Not surprisingly, given the way both sides came barging in at will, the townsfolk built not just one town wall but two, and what's left of them make a good walk. You'll enjoy the views of the river and the sea. And try Berwick cockles—not shellfish but old-fashioned peppermint candy.

On the other hand, if you're not visiting Berwick . . . go straight over the A1 ("Kentstone"), up a steady hill, then descend again. That brings you to a **T-junction** (47 miles). Turn **left** ("Lowick, Holborn"), then **right** at 48 miles ("Lowick, Wooler") on the **B6353**.

That takes you through **Lowick** (49 miles). Now follow signs across more sheep country, open and uninhabited, rolling gently, toward Wooler. On the skyline you can see the Cheviots. West and southwest of Wooler lies the Northumberland National Park. It reaches from Hadrian's Wall (see The Magic of Lindisfarne) in the south to the Cheviot Hills in the north. It's rich, silent, hillside country, little penetrated by roads.

Dotted around the moors are an ancient mystery. They're the "cup and ring" rocks, carved so that there's a cup hollowed from the rock surface. Once they must have held something, but now nobody knows what. Speculation has it that they date from the Bronze Age, but even that's not certain. The greatest concentration is on Doddington Moor, over an entire hillside to the east of Doddington.

This open road with occasional pine woods takes you through **Doddington** (55 miles) and into **WOOLER** (58 miles). It's an everyday sort of town, not impressive but important as a regional center. It'd be more impressive if the Scots hadn't knocked a lot of it down over the years and if what they left alone hadn't then burned down in the huge fires of 1722 and 1862.

At the **junction** with the **A697,** turn **left** ("Morpeth, town centre"). A few hundred yards farther, turn **left** on the **B6348** ("Belford, Chatton"). It's a good road, back out into open country. There are no houses, with a ridge of the Cheviots to the right. There's a changing mix of scrub, bushes and trees, with some longer climbs with occasional descents. Some of these ascents are tough, but rewarded by views into the valley.

After the toughest stretch, just out of Wooler, though, the road gets easier. It doesn't get flat, let alone downhill, but it does climb much more gently, undulating, to **Chatton** (63 miles).

Turn **right** in Chatton ("Chillingham, Alnwick") into **Chillingham** (64 miles). Chillingham Castle is signposted from the village and you'll pass it 1 mile later, on the left. It's a medieval fortress to which the Tudors added bits. There are furnished rooms, an Elizabethan topiary garden and a torture chamber. It's open daily except Tuesdays from May to September (06685-390 or 359).

Wild white cattle once roamed the hills of this area. There are none doing that now. In fact, only a handful survive. You can see some of them, saved by Chillingham Wild Cattle Association, in the estate office in Chillingham village (06685-213). Sadly, much of the herd has been dispersed, and you can see some of them at Whipsnade zoo in Bedfordshire (on the Chilterns and the Vale of Aylesbury route).

Now follow signs for Alnwick, through woods and copses. The contrast with the bleakness of a few miles ago is marked. You ride through the stone village of **Eglingham** (70 miles), with some eccentric hedge-carving (it's been trimmed into the shape of a pheasant) in the middle, and on into **ALNWICK** (77 miles).

You enter by way of the walls of Alnwick Castle. The town was a key stronghold in the days when the Scots and the English couldn't decide peacefully who should occupy this area which is spiritually Scottish but geographically English.

Alnwick Castle is a magnificent border fortress, now the home of the Duke of Northumberland. It includes a keep, armory and guard chamber, and works by Titian, Canaletto, Vandyke and others. The gardens are by Capability Brown—beautiful.

On the outside, the castle hasn't changed much since the 14th century. It was the birthplace of Harry Hotspur, so called because he was always on the move, "as if his spurs were hot." He created havoc against the Scots and became a national hero (to the English, anyway). But he came unstuck when he tried his luck against Henry IV—he was killed in the Battle of Shrewsbury and the estate and the castle were temporarily confiscated.

The castle is open daily from the end of April to the start of October, but not on Saturdays during May and September (0665-510777).

The Dukes of Northumberland's family symbol, the lion, is on the archway through which you'll ride to pass through the town. The other big symbol is the Percy Tenantry Column, sometimes also called the Farmers' Folly. It's 83 feet high. It went up in 1816, a time of great hardship in farming, because tenant farmers were grateful that they'd had their rents reduced. It gets its other name—Farmers' Folly—because legend has it that the Duke of Northumberland was so surprised to find his tenants had the cash to erect anything so elaborate that he promptly put their rents up again.

The center of Alnwick is warm, brown stone, with a gatehouse to the castle. The town is beautiful, and you'll find the tourist information office on the main road in the center, signposted. In late June each year, there's a medieval fair in the streets, with townspeople in costume, games and stalls. It's been held since 1291.

Leave by riding under the archway sign on the **A1068,** which takes you back to **ALNMOUTH** station (80 miles).

TOUR NO. 14

THE GENTLE VALE OF YORK
Central Yorkshire

Distance: 57 miles
Estimated time: 2 riding days
Terrain: Mainly easy
Maps: Ordnance Survey 100, 105
Rail: York (major rail junction and accessible from almost everywhere) is about 2 hours north of London (King's Cross), but check with British Rail about carrying your bike

This is the gentlest ride. York is the attraction, of course, but the Vale of York also has a quiet and restful charm. There are few hills, but there are spectacular ancient houses such as Castle Howard, haunting ruins like Rievaulx Abbey, and postcard villages such as Coxwold.

The route also skirts the North York Moors National Park, which invites separate inspection. The Forestry Commission—a national body concerned with commercial forestry, but often guardian of mature woods as well—encourages cycling on its land in the moors. Nearly all these routes are free, and some are signposted, but it has also opened toll routes through the moors for mountain bikers. You can get details from the commission at 42 Eastgate, Pickering, Yorkshire YO18 7DP.

I recommend you happily spend two days wandering along the full route, stopping and exploring the old houses and villages. However, if you wish to shorten the ride by 23 miles, you can leave off the loop to Rievaulx Abbey and do the shortened 34-mile ride in one day. There is also a 30-mile round-trip cycleway between York and Selby, for an additional day's ride in the area.

York to Helmsley: 31 Miles

YORK has been the home since 1945 of the annual cyclists' rally on the Knavesmire horse-racing course in the southwestern outskirts. Thousands camp there the weekend for a cycle exhibition, races, guided rides, a cyclists' service in the Minster (cathedral), and other events. It's usually held at the end of June (0483-417217, Monday-Friday 9:00 A.M. to 5:00 P.M.).

The city is 2,000 years old and exudes history wherever you go

within the city walls. The great industrial revolution which changed
so much of northern England passed it by, so that, if you ignore the
20th-century trappings, it still seems a medieval city.

The best way to see it is on the 90-minute walks that start from Exhibition Square. You can get details from either of the tourist information offices (see the appendix). Everything worth seeing is within
walking distance.

Sadly, York hasn't yet followed other cities' moves toward pedes-
trianization, so that most of the streets are overbusy. Frequently the
number of summer visitors just overpowers the traffic, however, so
that some parts of the city are effective no-go areas for drivers.

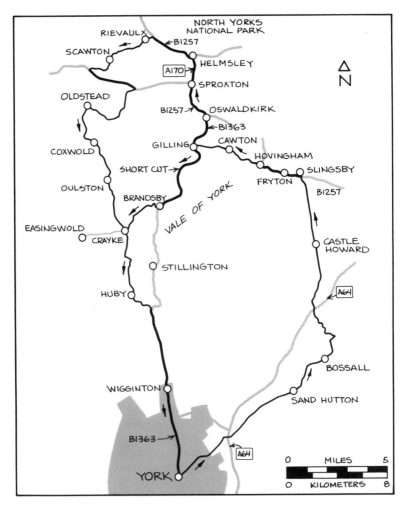

Castle Howard, "the biggest house in Yorkshire."

The Shambles and Stonegate are the most picturesque streets, but the city gem is the cathedral, here called the Minster. It was struck by lightning about ten years ago and parts caught fire and collapsed, but the repairs are complete and the cathedral is pretty much what it was.

The lightning strike followed a neighboring bishop's controversial remarks about the nature of God, sparking suggestions that the fire had been divine retribution.

The ride starts from the city and goes to the north. The start is the **ring road** just outside the center, at its **junction** with the **A1036** ("Scarborough"). **Cross the river** and turn **right** ("Heworth") and then immediately **left** into **Stockton Lane.** This is a tricky **junction** because it looks as though Stockton Lane's an ordinary domestic road.

Follow Stockton Lane past houses, cross the **A64** by bridge at 3 miles and on into open countryside. At 5 miles you'll come to a **T-junction;** turn **right** ("Warthill, Holtby"), pass under power cables and then, as the road swings right, you'll see Forest Farm on the left and a sign for a public bridleway. Turn **left** through the gate where it says "Forest Farm road only" and it'll bring you on to a **leafy lane,** where you turn **right** through the trees at 7½ miles and carry on to **Sand Hutton** (8½ miles).

At 9 miles, turn **right** ("Bossall") by a war memorial and follow signs to **Bossall** (11 miles). Go through the village to a **T-junction** (12 miles), where you turn **right** toward Howsham and Malton. Another **T-junction** follows ¼ mile later; turn **left** ("Barton-le-Willows, Crambe") and immediately **right** down a gated road ("Crambe").

You'll **cross the railroad** 1 mile later and then find a **crossroads** 1 mile later; turn **left** ("Malton, York"). That brings you to the **junction** with the **A64,** on which you turn **left** and immediately **right** ("Whitwell-on-the-hill"). Take care because you're crossing a busy highway beyond the brow of a hill.

You'll see a sign on this **junction** for Kirkham Priory ½ mile away. There are only ruins left, and lawns which stretch to the river Derwent, but what's left is attractive enough. It housed Augustinian canons back in the 12th century; legend says a chap called Walter L'Espec built it after his only son died in a hunting accident. The bit of stone cross at the entrance is supposed to be where it happened.

This **lane** takes you back before long to the **A64.** Just before you get there, look on the left for two old gate pillars (16 miles) and a **bumpy unsurfaced road** that leads between them. That's the road you take.

(It's bumpy and, if you prefer not to take it, you can carry on to the **A64** and turn **left** toward Welburn and you'll rejoin the route in 1 mile or so. The track is ridable, though, and more enjoyable than the main road, which is the principal highway between north Yorkshire and the seaside towns of Scarborough and Filey.)

After ½ mile on the track, you pass between more old gateposts and ahead you'll get your first sight of the impressive **CASTLE**

HOWARD. At the gateposts, the route splits; take the **left-hand fork,** alongside the trees. It's an enjoyable old cart road with a grassy ridge down the middle.

Before long, you reach a **conventional road** (17 miles), at which you turn **right** onto what, from its straightness, looks like a **Roman road.** Had you taken the other route round, you'll rejoin at the first **crossroads,** at which point you turn **right** ("Castle Howard, Slingsby").

Take that **long, straight road,** through a gatehouse in the castle wall, through a castellated wall, over a humped-back bridge and on through a second, more impressive gatehouse (18 miles) where, straight ahead, you'll see an obelisk like Cleopatra's Needle on the banks of the Thames in London.

Castle Howard is, you won't be surprised to hear once you've seen it, the largest house in Yorkshire. But that belittles its impact. Work started on it in 1700 and didn't finish until 1737, by which time they'd spent $110,000. It's a wealth of furniture and paintings, including Rubens, Vandyke, Reynolds and Canaletto—and Holbein's classic portrait of Henry VIII. The grounds run to 1,000 acres. It is open from April until the end of October.

The Shambles in York; you can still picture how it was in medieval times.

Should you have seen it, the house and grounds were the setting for the TV series "Brideshead Revisited." They were home for George Howard, a gargantuan and kaftan-wearing millionaire who was until recently chairman of the BBC.

The road carries on past the main entrance, through rolling parkland with pleasing views over the Vale of York, past the **Slingsby** sign (22 miles) but not into the village itself. Turn **left** instead on the **B1257** ("Helmsley"). You'll see a sign here, too, for Nunnington Hall. It was the home of Robert Huicke, physician to the royals—the man who told Elizabeth I that she'd never have children and Henry VIII, presumably, why he suffered indigestion.

Go into **Hovingham** (23 miles) along High Street, pass the pub and the church and go on to the Spa Garage, which has an attractive ford beside it. Go through the **ford** and then **left** by some beautiful stone cottages alongside the stream. When you get to Hovingham Farm, follow the signs to the **right** saying "rights of way" and then, at a split, follow the path marked "Ebor Way; bridleway only, no vehicles."

Curiously, next to this sign is another: "Sheep will graze this cemetery the first week in each month."

Follow the **bridleway,** which is ridable, for 2 miles to **Cawton** (25 miles), passing Hovingham Spa on the way. The path emerges at Spring Farm Cottage; go straight ahead and on to **Gilling** (26 miles) to meet the **B1363** in front of the Fairfax Arms.

You now have a choice. You can go on a loop to give you a view of the North York Moors National Park and the dramatic ruins of Rievaulx Abbey, or you can go left to **Crayke** and cut the ride short by one day (23 miles).

If you're going on the loop, carry on reading here. If you're not, skip through to mention of Crayke and carry on from there.

Turn **right** at the Fairfax Arms onto the **B1363** ("Helmsley"), through **Oswaldkirk** (28 miles) and up a hill to a **T-junction,** where you turn **left** ("Helmsley, Sproxton") onto the **B1257**. It's this road that forms the boundary of the national park. You'll reach **Sproxton** (30 miles) to turn **right** on the **A170** ("Scarborough, Stokesley"). The gateway opposite you leads into Duncombe Park, now a school but once the home of Thomas Duncombe, who built the temples that overlook Rievaulx Abbey.

Ride into **Helmsley** (31 miles) and cross the river Rye. A hundred yards further turn **left** on the **B1257** ("Stokesley, Rievaulx Abbey"). Rievaulx Abbey is a considerable tourist attraction in these parts and Helmsley suffers from the hangers-on of the tourist industry. Still, it's not totally spoiled and the prettiness of the original market town is still obvious.

There's a footpath from your left to Helmsley Castle, which seems to have had a peaceful life, having given in to Cromwell after a three-month siege and consequently not having been knocked about too much.

Helmsley falls at roughly the right distance for a night's stop. You should find overnight accommodation without too much difficulty. If you don't like the idea of staying in a touristified center, look out for small bed-and-breakfast houses along the route.

Helmsley to York: 26 Miles

Now follow signs for Rievaulx Abbey. As you get nearer, you have a choice. The first track goes to the terrace and temples (open April through October) and the second down Rievaulx Bank into **Rievaulx** (33 miles), with the abbey on your left.

Back in the 13th century, this area was a wilderness. Twelve Cistercians moved in in 1131 and turned it into one of the country's most spectacular religious buildings. Three hundred years later, there were 140 monks and 500 lay brothers, which was so unwieldy that they began knocking some of the buildings down again.

Legend says Rievaulx spellbound Dorothy Wordsworth, got Turner painting, and made Cowper want to stay forever. It's a ruin now, of course, but open to visitors.

Pass the abbey and after ½ mile turn **right** over a bridge ("Scawton, Old Byland") into a **lane** which I enjoyed. It's wooded, with overhanging branches that make it dark even on a sunny day. It takes you out of the Rievaulx valley and into **Scawton** (37 miles). Go on to the **A170** and turn **right** ("Thirsk"). Pass the Hambleton Inn ¼ mile later and turn **left** ("White Horse Bank"). Pass the gliding club and enjoy the views south over the York plain.

Now comes a breathtaking descent. It's a one-in-four drop and if your eyes aren't watering too much, you might still notice the remains of names painted on the road, all the way down. They were there to encourage riders in the Tour of Britain—which came *up* the climb.

The road snakes. On the outside of one bend there's a parking lot. Stop, look back, and you'll see the tail, legs and body of the white horse, carved into the hillside, which gives the road its name. "Bank" is simply a north-of-England alternative to "hill."

Shapes cut into hillsides are an occasional feature of rural life in England, particularly where the underlying surface is chalk. This horse—which you'll see better from the valley—is remarkable only because it's there, and there are better ones. Among the best are another white horse, at Uffington in Oxfordshire, and an impressively rampant man at Cerne Abbas in Dorset.

There's a **T-junction** at the bottom. Turn **left,** pass through **Oldstead** (43 miles), with Byland Abbey on your left after the village. The abbey's in ruins now, but it's open to visitors.

Quiet stone villages and a chance to splash through the river are features of the Vale of York. This is your route through Hovingham.

Turn **right** opposite the abbey to **Coxwold** (45 miles). At the **cross-roads** on the village edge, go **left.** But spare a moment to go the other way, into the village, which with its honey-colored stone looks as if it's been moved from the Cotswolds. The whole village is attractive, but on the northern side you'll find Shandy Hall. It's smaller than the name suggests, and remarkable more for its story than its appearance.

It was the home of a wacky parson called Laurence Sterne. There was no vicarage in the village, so he moved into this building and called it Shandy Hall. At that time, shandy was a dialect word meaning eccentric. Sterne lived there for eight years after 1760, writing novels and dying of tuberculosis. In 1969, his body was brought back from London, where its tombstone had the lines:

> *Sterne was the Man who with gigantic stride*
> *Mow'd down luxuriant follies far and wide*

If you call at the hall, which is now headquarters of the Shandy Trust, you can find out more from the curators, Kenneth and Julia Monkman. It's open on Wednesday afternoons in summer, or by arrangement.

Having visited the village, retrace to the **crossroads** and follow the road marked Oulston and Malton. Coxwold now has one last treat. The road swings as you leave and on the left is a lake with lilies and a warning to beware ducks. There are stone walls and green walls, with the remains of Newburgh Priory farther to the left. The priory's a private home, but it's open on Wednesdays in summer.

Carry on to **Oulston** (49 miles), a pretty village of stone houses and hanging flowers, and continue to **Crayke,** where those not taking the 23-mile loop to Rievaulx Abbey can take up the route again. Turn **right** in the village ("Easingwold, York"), **left** at a **T-junction** ("Stillington"), and ¼ mile later turn **right** ("Huby, Sutton-on-the-Forest").

Go into **Huby** and watch carefully to the right. Just after the road swings left and then straightens, you'll see a narrow, unsignposted and **unsurfaced road** on the **right,** between houses. It runs between houses set back from the road, skirts a duckfield, and then takes on a better surface after some initial potholes.

Leave the houses behind and carry on between open fields. The surface improves until eventually it becomes an ordinary lane. After 1 mile or so, at 53 miles and just after the Jacobean Plainville Hall, it makes a **T-junction.** Turn **left** ("Wigginton") to reach the **B1363** and turn **right** to **YORK** (57 miles).

That completes the ride, but before you head back to the city, you'll see a sign for Beningborough Hall, an old house owned by the National Trust. It's 5½ miles out of the city, three miles west of Shipton, a tall, rectangular building of two stories. The most remarkable point is a vast staircase with treads seven feet wide. The whole thing is intricately carved—intricacy is the theme of the whole house. In 1978, the National Portrait Gallery opened a permanent exhibition here of 17th- and 18th-century portraits.

York-to-Selby Cycleway: 30 Miles

There's another ride from York—a traffic-free 30-mile round-trip along a converted railroad. Cars, motorcycles and mopeds aren't allowed, and horse-riders can use only part of it.

The line closed in September 1983 after sinking land at Selby coalfield ended fast trains. A cycling charity called Sustrans (Sustainable Transport) acquired the land as far as Selby and began work in June 1985. The completed ride was opened by the former world champion, Beryl Burton, in November 1987. The path could eventually run into the city center.

You'll find the route signed from the center. It starts between the race course and the river Ouse, near the end of **Bishopthorpe Road.** From there it passes through or near **Naburn, Escrick, Riccall** and **Barlby** on its way to **Selby** (15 miles).

Sadly, this is rich coal country and three power-stations spoil the countryside.

At the Selby end, it starts at **Barlby Bank,** alongside the Ouse. You can ride alongside the river on a cycle track and pick up the converted railroad near its **junction** with the **A19.** Indeed, part of the route uses the former A19.

Selby's worth a visit for its cathedral-size abbey, built in 1069. Look for the Washington Window, high in the choir. John de Washington was a relative of George Washington and you'll see that the window, made in the 14th century, has the Washington family arms, the model for the Stars and Stripes.

The abbey's open from 9:00 A.M. every day, closing some time between 4:00 P.M. and 7:00 P.M. according to the season.

Once you return to York, think how the city so nearly changed British history. Guy Fawkes, whose celebrated attempt to blow up the Houses of Parliament brought the annual November 5 bonfire-and-firework celebrations, came from York. Sir Thomas Kynvet, who found the gunpowder, lived in Escrick Park.

From This Ride to Lincoln and The Wolds: 70 Miles

You can take a train from York to Lincoln, or you can ride. The ride isn't one of the most picturesque you'll have made, but it is at least flat—frequently very flat. Main roads are unavoidable at first, but it's possible to take quieter direct roads from about half-distance. The total distance is a little short of 70 miles, only a few of which have a great deal to commend them. Take the train if you're pushed for time.

Leave **York** on the cycleway to **Selby** (15 miles) just described. Then go southeast on the **A1041** to **Snaith** and on to the **junction** with the **A614.** Turn **right** there and follow the A614 toward Thorne and Doncaster.

The A614 goes into **Thorne** and runs to a **junction** with the **M180.** Go straight ahead at this **roundabout** onto the **A18,** which at this point absorbs the A614. In less than 1 mile there's a lane to the **left.** If you get as far as where the A18 and the A614 split again, you've gone just a little too far.

Turn **left** into that **lane,** which then runs parallel but a few hundred yards south of the M180, before swinging away southeast at **Sandtoft.** Stay on this lane to **Epworth,** go over the **A161** to **Owston Ferry,** ride through the village to the river Trent, turn **right** and ride alongside the river for several miles to **West Stockwith**, after which you'll come to the **A161** again. Turn left to **GAINSBOROUGH.**

Leave Gainsborough to the south on the **Newark road** and ride a couple of miles to **Lea.** Turn **left** there on the **B1241** through **Willingham-by-Stow** to **Sturton-by-Stow.** Turn **left** there to **Brattleby** and then turn **right** and **south** again on the **B1398** to **LINCOLN.**

TOUR NO. 15

LINCOLN AND THE WOLDS
Lincolnshire

Distance: 65 miles
Estimated time: 2 riding days
Terrain: Flat, with some moderate and occasionally stiff hills in the middle
Maps: Ordnance Survey 121, 122
Rail: Lincoln is about 2 hours north of London (King's Cross), but check with British Rail about carrying your bike; some trains are direct

The Lincolnshire Wolds is a range of hills recognized as an Area of Outstanding Natural Beauty, with the preservation that that implies. There are sleepy villages and history going back hundreds of years.

The first and last parts of the ride are flat, through some of Britain's richest arable country. It's an area not of drama but of arching and endless skies above fields of blowing corn. The Wolds then creep up on the horizon, and suddenly you're into hills of moderate height but with occasional stiff climbs. There is sweeping downland beauty.

The ride is 65 miles long if you start and finish in Lincoln, but you could cut out the least spectacular 30 miles by starting and finishing in Horncastle.

Lincoln to Old Bolingbroke: 31 Miles

LINCOLN is a Roman city in which William the Conqueror built a castle in 1068; it still stands. The city's most famous feature is the 900-year-old three-towered cathedral, which is a tough climb from the city center. You can cycle up on the main road but a more attractive way is the pedestrian route up the aptly named Steep Hill. Look for medieval shops and Jew's House (1170), now a restaurant and beauty salon. West of the cathedral is the castle, open daily except winter Sundays.

Leave Lincoln by the **B1188** ("Cherry Willingham") and follow through **Fiskerton** to **Short Ferry** (7 miles), and cross the Old River Witham. If you have a headwind, the coming few miles will prove tougher than the climbs that follow. The hedges have been grubbed out for what the locals call (but Canadians wouldn't recognize as) prairie-farming.

At 9 miles, **cross** an abandoned **railroad** and a **stream** to the **junction** with the **B1202.** Turn **left** ("Kingthorpe, Wragby"), then straight on ½ mile later onto a **minor road** ("Minting, Baumber").

The country undulates but it's still open, green in February but brilliant gold from the corn of high summer. In the middle of all this is a sign saying it's a Neighborhood Watch area—mutual crime prevention—although nobody here has a neighbor less than half a mile away!

Keep following signs for Minting until, at 13 miles, you find signs for Wispington and Baumber. Keep going to **Wispington.** There, in the middle of nowhere, you'll find an unusual L-shaped monument on the right with a metal model of an agricultural plow. It's in the grounds of a large house and carries the flags of 24 countries and the legend "Let peace till the fields." It marks the 31st world plowing championship in 1984.

Soon afterward is the **junction** with the **B1190.** Take that road straight ahead, past the thatched cottages of **Thimbleby** (18 miles). Turn **right** outside the village at the Durham Ox pub into **Mill Lane** ("Thornton"). The map shows a windmill, but the sails have gone.

If you were to detour just 1 mile to **Horncastle** (Banovallum to the Romans, and bits of the city walls remain), you'll see pikes and scythes used during the Civil War. The main route later goes within a couple of miles of the battlefield, where the two sides met while the Royalists were on their way to the castle at Old Bolingbroke.

Turn **right** and **left** straight after the mill, join the **B1191** and go into **Thornton.** A mile later, after the road swings right (21 miles), **cross** a dismantled **railroad** and turn **left** on to a **minor road** ("Roughton, Kirkby-on-Bain").

This is the valley of the Old River Bain and the disused Horncastle canal, to your left. Go through **Roughton** (22 miles) and carry on to the next **lane on the left** and take that and the **A153** into **Haltham** (23 miles).

From Haltham you can detour 4 miles south to Tattershall Castle. The five-storey keep is one of the best medieval brick buildings. It was built for the Lord Treasurer of England in about 1440. There are good views from the 100-foot tower. It belongs to the National Trust (0526-42543).

In Haltham, turn **right** ("Wood Enderby, Moorby"). Follow signs for **Moorby** (26 miles). You're now close to the hills of the Wolds. Go through the village on the **B1183,** then straight on at Manor Farm to Miningsby. This road is also signposted to Claxby Pluckacre, a wonderful name but no actual village.

There are two gates on this road. Don't worry if they're closed—they're for cattle. Pass through and leave the gates as you found them.

Go on into **Miningsby** (29 miles) and follow signs to **Hareby.** There's an attractive pond on the left—turn **right** there to Old

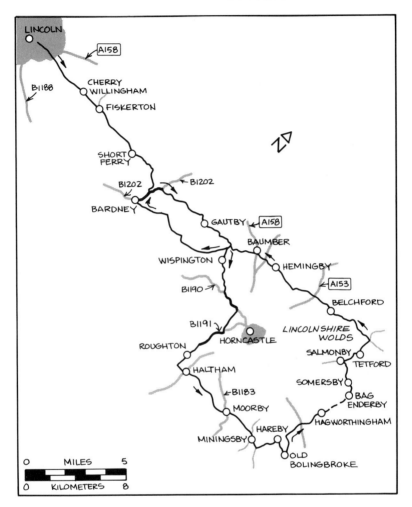

Bolingbroke. As you go down the hill out of Hareby, look for a downhill left-hand bend. There's a white, thatched cottage on the left and, opposite it, a thatched lych-gate with a conical roof. You'd expect it to lead into a church, where roofed gates protected coffin-bearers waiting for the parson. This, though, seems to be a private folly, the entrance to a garden.

Go on into **Old Bolingbroke** (31 miles) and explore a charming village. Old Bolingbroke sounds like a paunchy gent from Cromwell's time, and well he might have been. There was a proper castle here, built by John of Gaunt (Henry IV's father), until Cromwell's soldiers knocked it down in 1643 after winning the battle of Winceby. What remains fell into a sorry state but it's now been tidied a bit. Look by the church doorway for two worn, stone heads; they're supposed to be of John of Gaunt's parents, Edward III and Queen Philippa. Old Bolingbroke is where Henry IV was born in 1367 and there are 18th-century houses and shops.

It's only a small village, but it's also in a tourist area. It's a charmingly rural spot to break your journey, but it's wise to try to arrange accommodation in advance. The tourist offices in Lincoln will be able to suggest ways of contacting local bed-and-breakfast houses and small hotels. Alternatively, you could detour 3 miles into the small town of Spilsby, although it would still be better to book in advance.

Old Bolingbroke to Lincoln: 34 Miles

Leave Old Bolingbroke by the village green. Keep the war memorial to your left and go straight across ("Asgarby, Horncastle"), past Ivy Chimneys Antiques and out of the village on the puff-making climb of Horncastle Hill.

From the neighboring village of East Keal, you can look southeast to Boston on a fine day and see the inelegantly named Stump, or tower, of St. Botolph's church. It's the largest parish church in England, but more significant is that the town gave its name to a rather larger place in Massachusetts.

Follow signs into **Hagworthingham** (34 miles), taking care on a narrow descent and a watersplash. If the water's deep, there's a bridge.

On the entrance to Hagworthingham, turn **right** before the church into **Manor Road,** go up the hill, following the twists, and cross the **A158** ("Harington, Brinkhill").

A few hundred yards after the A158, you'll see a **minor road** to the left, marked "Bridle road unfit for motorists." It's roughly surfaced most of the way, and there's a bridge across a stream. The whole path section is about 1¼ miles and takes you into the curiously named **Bag Enderby** (37 miles). On the right is the church of St. Margaret's, where Queen Victoria's poet laureate, Alfred Tennyson, worshipped until he was 28. Tennyson's father was the rector there. (The Isle of Wight tour crosses Tennyson Down, where the poet lived and went walking.)

Go up through Bag Enderby and then turn **left** at a small green with a lightning-blasted tree. Go through **Somersby** to **Salmonby,** and then right into **Tetford** (40 miles).

Salmonby, in the old rectory, is where Tennyson was born at Christmastime in 1809. He's buried in Westminster Abbey, but there are monuments to him in the church. There's also a statue of him outside Lincoln cathedral. "Maud," of the poems, lived at Harrington Hall, near Spilsby.

Go through Tetford, turn **left** and then **right** to continue in the same direction. Climb Tetford hill and turn **left** ("Belchford, Oxcombe") onto the **Blueston Heath Road.** There are now spectacular views to the left.

Take the **first road left** into **Belchford** (43 miles), straight through, cross the **A153** (44 miles), through **Hemingby,** turn **right, left, right again** on the **A158** and then immediately **left** ("Wispington, Bardney") to continue in the same direction.

At the **T-junction** 1 mile later, you'll meet the road you were on just before you reached Wispington and its plowing monument.

Follow signs to Bardney through that same open, rolling country. Go into **Bardney** (56 miles), turn **right** at the **junction** by the war memorial ("Lincoln etc.") and then immediately **right** onto the **B1202, Wragby Road.** It's easy to go left by mistake, because it's not clearly signposted.

Follow the B1202 for 1 mile and you'll find the road on which you rode out. Turn **left** over the stream and the bridge over the abandoned railroad and retrace through **Short Ferry** (58 miles), **Fiskerton** (60 miles) and **Cherry Willingham** (62 miles) to **Lincoln** (65 miles).

From This Ride to Beautiful Norfolk: 65 Miles or 105 Miles

The closest point of the Norfolk circular route is King's Lynn, which is halfway round. Unfortunately, there are only intermittent attractive areas between Lincoln and King's Lynn and more than 90 percent of the rest is table-flat, bleak arable land with a paucity of trees and general shelter. The area was drained from the sea by the Dutch several hundred years ago and, frankly, looks it.

It's possible to reach King's Lynn from Lincoln by rail, but only with much journeying out of your way and several changes of train. So here, first, is a 65-mile direct route along smaller roads. And after that, a longer, curving route which makes a worthwhile 105-mile one-way tour in itself.

The direct route: Go south out of Lincoln in the general direction of the soccer ground (ask for directions). Still within the built-up area, look for signs for the **B1188** and follow it through Branston, Metheringham and Riskington into Sleaford (the last few miles are on the **A153**).

If by mistake you can't find the right road leaving Lincoln, the **A15** is equally direct but a little busier. Both roads roll gently up and down. Either way, it's about 20 miles to **Sleaford.**

The next stage is to **Spalding,** about another 20 miles. Of these, the first 10 are pleasant enough but the final 10 are flat and monotonous.

Rolling and endless—the grace and quiet beauty of Lincolnshire Wolds
(Lincolnshire County Council)

There's a railroad station on the southern edge of Sleaford (only a small town) with a service to Spalding.

The riding route is to go south through Sleaford to the railroad crossing. Cross the tracks and go **left** (if you check the map, it's the road that goes straight ahead, in effect) and ignore the A15 and A153 signs.

This road runs around some old industrial buildings and after a sharp **left** and a sharp **right** emerges into countryside. This is **Mareham Lane** and it's an old Roman road, almost straight and almost due south. Cross the A52 after 5 miles at Threekingham (say *Threkking'm*) and then, 1 mile later, turn **left** at a **crossroads** to Billingborough. It's here that the flatness begins.

Turn **right** in Billingborough on the **B1177** and ride for less than 1 mile. To the left (if you get to Pointon you've gone too far) is a lane running due east. Take that **lane** and ride 5 miles toward Gosberton. But ignore Gosberton and go instead toward Gosberton Clough (say *Cloff*). When you get to the **B1397** on the edge of the village, turn **right** and then **left** and go through Northgate to meet the **A151** near Pinchbeck West. Turn **left** on the A151 to **Spalding.**

Spalding is a difficult town to navigate, partly because it's split by a river and second because the signposting is haphazard at best. The road you want starts on the other side of the river from the town center. You'll almost certainly have to ask, although there are signs. It's the **B1165** to Sutton St. James. There are now another 25 miles to King's Lynn.

Halfway between Spalding and Sutton St. James is the tiny Fenland village of Whaplode St. Catherine. It's unremarkable except that, in a collection of cottages and outhouses, there's the Rutland Cottage Music Museum (open in the summer months). It's a bizarre assembly of old gramophones, obscure musical instruments, fairground equipment and a unique puppet theater. It was started as a hobby by a policeman called Ray Tunnicliff, who was injured during a demo and retired early. From there, things rather took over.

So, go into Sutton St. James and from there, still on the **B1165,** to Tydd St. Giles (say *Tidd*). Now turn **left** to Tydd Gote, cross the A1101 and follow the canal to Sutton Bridge. Now turn **right** over the swing **bridge** and ride 10 unavoidable miles along the busy **A17** to **King's Lynn** (unavoidable, that is, except that if you turn into West Lynn just before the main town, there's a tiny ferry across the river; it saves you no time at all, but it does avoid several miles of busy road and it's good fun in its own right. It's signposted from West Lynn village.)

Now the longer, scenic route: Leave **Lincoln** on the **A46** to Newark. After 1 mile or so, you'll cross the river Witham. Take the **next road left,** to North Hykeham and follow to South Hykeham, Haddington, Thurlby and Bossingham (about 10 miles).

Go through Bassingham to Carlton-le-Moorland but swing **left** on the village outskirts to Brant Broughton. Cross the A17 on the far side of the village to **Stragglethorpe** (15 miles) and go on into Brandon. This is the end of the flat section.

Turn **left** in Brandon to Hough-on-the-Hill and follow signs southeast to Belton and Grantham. Belton House is one of the great stately homes of Britain and well worth a visit. It stands in hundreds of acres of parkland and deer park and, as you'd expect, can get busy. If you have time, there's another wonderful old building 10 miles to the southwest, on the other side of Grantham (the birthplace of Mrs. Thatcher and once branded the most boring town in Britain, incidentally). It's Belvoir Castle (say *Beever*), which stands proudly on a wooded hill overlooking the beautiful Vale of Belvoir. Well worth the detour.

Grantham (about 25 miles) will find you a roof for the night, after which you should carry on south on the **A52** and continue south on the **B1174,** which joins the A1 at Little Ponton.

Keep off the A1, which is fast and busy, but turn **left** just before it through what little there is of Little Ponton, then **left** again over the Witham. The railroad follows; go under the bridge, and then take the **right** turn to Woodnook (all this in less than 1 mile). Now turn **right** and southeast on the **B6403** (Ermine Street, an old Saxon and Roman road; the Romans, incidentally, built from town to town—the Saxons, knowing that roads bring mobile thieves, established their villages safely to one side).

Keep on the **B6403,** cross the A1 and go into **Colsterworth** (35 miles). It was here that Isaac Newton sat and received an apple on his head, stunning him into realization of the law of gravity. Woolsthorpe Manor, where it's supposed to have happened, is on the edge of the village. The apple tree, if it ever existed, is no longer there.

Manor is too grand a description of this homely cottage in which Newton was born in 1642 and to which he retreated twice because of the plague in London. The house is owned by the National Trust and open to visitors (although you'll have to remove cleated cycling shoes for the sake of the floor).

Go due south from Colsterworth, not on the B6403 but on the **minor road** to South Witham. Turn **left** in the village and ride to **Castle Bytham** (45 miles), where the castle's remains stand to one edge of the village. Turn **right** in the village and follow signs to **Stamford** (53 miles).

Stamford is one of the great towns of Britain and the country's first designated conservation areas. It's built almost entirely of stone, with soaring church spires and interesting nooks and crannies. To the southern edge, across the Welland, is the ancient George Hotel, where stage coaches changed horses on the route from London to York, and where an ancient wooden beam still spans the road.

Ride through the town, over the Welland past the George, and then turn **left** into a partly obscured road, the **B1443,** signposted to Burleigh House and Barnack. Burleigh House is another of the romantic old stately piles in which this area is so rich. Had the Nazis won the war, it would have become Hermann Goering's private residence and one imagines there was a short future for Luftwaffe pilots who hit it instead of the diesel factories in nearby Peterborough.

You can visit from spring to fall. In summer it's the venue of the Burleigh international horse trials, at which Princess Anne is a regular visitor and her former husband, Mark Phillips, is course designer. At one stage, incidentally, they were fond of visiting the most expensive restaurant in the area between competitions; to the astonishment of local rural opinion, they told friends it was "amusingly cheap."

From **Burleigh,** continue along the **B1443** to Barnack, Bainton and Helpston (birthplace and burial site of the peasants' poet, John Clare) to cross the new road and enter Glinton. Continue along the B1443 to **Peakirk** (65 miles), where the Wildfowl Trust keeps hundreds of breeds of water birds, some of them rare. Visitors are welcome.

At the far end of Peakirk, leave the B1443 and turn **left** on a **minor road** northwest to three of six Deeping villages. Three of them have joined up, so you'll cross the Welland by a narrow hump-back bridge at Deeping Gate. Turn **right** to Deeping St. James and follow the **B1165** through flat country to **Crowland** (about 75 miles). Here there are two remarkable features. The first is an ancient raised triangular bridge over nothing at all in the town center. An inscription will explain why. And the second is the gaunt and partly ruined abbey, which is worth a look (although the view is now impaired by the intrusion of equally gaunt but less attractive modern housing).

Leave Crowland southeastward, cross the A1073 Spalding road and go on another 1½ miles to the hamlet of Nene Terrace. Turn **left** off the **B1040** and ride alongside one of the area's many drainage rivers almost due east. In 2 miles the road becomes the **B1167,** turns **sharp left** and crosses a disused railroad to a **T-junction.** Turn **right** through Throckenholt to **Parson Drove** (about 85 miles). Turn **left** through Parson Drove and follow to **Wisbech** (90 miles).

Wisbech is a workaday, inland port devoted to the canning of fruit. The parallel roads along the Nene, though, are beautiful and Georgian, especially so on the north side. Ask for The Brinks and, while you're there, visit Peckover House. It's a pleasant Georgian townhouse owned by the National Trust, with a small but restful garden behind it—an oasis of rest after a long, flat ride.

Leave Wisbech on the **A47** toward King's Lynn but turn **left** before the end of town to West Walton. Like many churches in this area of the Fens, West Walton's is enormous (at one time, before the area was drained, the church would have been the one secure refuge from flooding). Unlike others, though, the tower the villagers wanted to build was too much for the church to bear. Had they joined it to the church, the weight would have pulled the main building down into the marshy soil. So, determined they'd still have a massive tower, they built it separately and there it stands to this day. The other churches along this route are impressive, too.

Go on through Walpole St. Andrew to join the **A12** at Terrington St. Clement. Turn **right** on the A12 to **King's Lynn** and you're on the final miles of the direct route detailed previously. Remember that you can still use the ferry across from West Lynn to the main town (about 105 miles).

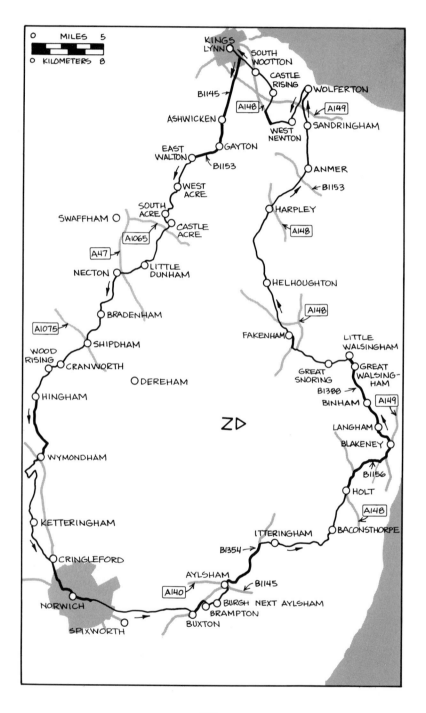

MILES 0 — 5
KILOMETERS 0 — 8

KINGS LYNN
SOUTH WOOTTON
CASTLE RISING
WOLFERTON
B1145
A148
A149
ASHWICKEN
WEST NEWTON
SANDRINGHAM
EAST WALTON
GAYTON
B1153
ANMER
WEST ACRE
B1153
SOUTH ACRE
SWAFFHAM
CASTLE ACRE
HARPLEY
A1065
A148
A47
NECTON
LITTLE DUNHAM
HELHOUGHTON
BRADENHAM
A148
A1075
SHIPDHAM
FAKENHAM
WOOD RISING
CRANWORTH
LITTLE WALSINGHAM
HINGHAM
DEREHAM
GREAT SNORING
GREAT WALSINGHAM
B1388
BINHAM
A149
LANGHAM
BLAKENEY
WYMONDHAM
B1156
HOLT
KETTERINGHAM
A148
BACONSTHORPE
CRINGLEFORD
ITTERINGHAM
B1354
NORWICH
AYLSHAM
B1145
A140
BURGH NEXT AYLSHAM
BRAMPTON
SPIXWORTH
BUXTON

152

BEAUTIFUL NORFOLK
North-Central Norfolk

Distance: 135 miles
Estimated time: 3 riding days
Terrain: Gentle
Rail: Norwich is about 1½ hours from London (Liverpool Street)
Maps: Ordnance Survey 132, 133, 134, 144

Norfolk, like Cornwall, ought to be another country. Outsiders, distinguished by their lack of the rolling, quizzical local accent, are still referred to as "furriners."

The country is gentle and pastoral but beautiful enough for sizable parts to be designated an official Area of Outstanding Natural Beauty, with the protection that that achieves.

You'll see the graceful beauty of Norwich, the rustic waterside village of Blakeney with its seals and rare birds, the ancient shrine village of Walsingham, the dotty abbey of Wymondham, and all the wonderful countryside between them.

You'll see churches with round towers (local flint wouldn't build into squares), find curious American connections, and pay a visit to the Queen.

Norwich to Walsingham: 43 Miles

The ride starts from **NORWICH** station. Leave the station and turn **right** and then **right again** into **Thorpe Road,** which runs up alongside the station. This is the Norwich inner ring road. Follow the ring-road signs to go across **three roundabouts.**

Then, after the third, take the first turn **right** (3½ miles) into **Spixworth Road**. There's a short stretch of central reservation (median) at this point, so you'll either have to push your bike across it or ride around its end.

Go out through **Spixworth** (5 miles), which is little more than an outlying suburb, to **Buxton** (11 miles). There's a sad reminder here of how medicine wasn't always what we now take for granted. On the wall of the chancel of the village church is a plaque to a little girl who died from attempts to inoculate her against smallpox.

It says: "To Mary Ann Kent, who died under inoculation on the tenth day of March 1773 in the fourth year of her age. This much lamented child was in the highest state of health and her mental powers began to open and promise fairest fame, when her fond parents deluded by prevalent custom suffered the rough officious hand of art to wound the flourishing root of nature and rob the little innocent of the gracious gift of life."

Feeling saddened, perhaps, go on through the village and then cross the **B1354 Aylsham road,** signposted "Brampton, Tuttington." In other words, although we're headed for Aylsham, ignore the Aylsham signs.

At the **Brampton** sign, the cross which shows two fish kissing each other actually says "Brantuna." It comes soon after a railroad bridge. Turn **left** at the sign ("Marlsham, Aylsham") and then 50 yards later turn **right** into **The Street.**

Carry on to the end of the road, round a dogleg which takes you around a charming little church with a round tower, and at the end of the road you'll see a farmyard, with a path running alongside a barn.

Go straight on along that **path.** It's only about 30 yards long. At the end of it is an **unsurfaced track** through trees. The track has the legal status of a footpath. Push your bike along it and over a wooden bridge across a stream. At the far side, a few hundred yards later, you'll rejoin the road alongside a church in **Burgh next Aylsham** (13 miles).

Turn **left** in the village toward Aylsham. To the left along this road is the narrow-gauge railroad between Aylsham and Wroxham. It was a full-scale track until British Rail closed it some years ago. Businessmen then converted it into a tourist attraction with steam trains, but it's had a checkered history and its future isn't certain. Trains, mainly steam, run spring to fall (0263-733858).

Go on toward Aylsham and, at the **junction** with the **A140** (unsignposted), go straight over ("Norfolk Highways DLO Area 1") to the center of **AYLSHAM** (16 miles).

Turn **right** on the **B1145** ("Bawdeswell, Saxthorpe"). That takes you round the side of the Black Boy Inn (a pub from the Queen Anne era) and you'll start seeing signs for the great Jacobean showpiece of Blickling Hall, on the **B1354.** You'll also pass a quaint, thatched-roof village water pump.

Continue on the B1354, **cross** an abandoned railroad by **bridge** (17 miles) and then carry on just a little farther along the B1354. The entrance to **Blickling Hall** is set among glorious and very English gardens. In the grounds—and it astonishes you when you come across it—is a 45-foot geometrically perfect pyramid, built in 1793. It houses the remains of the Earl of Buckingham and his two wives. It's also surrounded by gardens and a park. The hall is open from the end of March to the end of October. It belongs to the National Trust (0263-733084).

Retrace your route to the **B1354** and, a few hundred yards before the bridge, take the turn toward Ingworth and then **left** 1 mile later ("Blickling Lake"). This is a **narrow lane,** wide enough for three cyclists, and it stays like this for quite a few miles now. At a bend just down the lane, you'll find the entrance to Blickling Lake on your left.

Carry on along the lane, though, if you're not visiting the lake. Go straight on at the first **junction** ("Matlaske, Holt"), over the river and into **Itteringham** (22 miles). There's a sign down this lane, to the left, to Mannington Hall, which is open every day from Easter to October from 9:00 A.M. (026387-4175). The gardens surround a medieval moated manor house, with lake, shrubs and rose gardens.

Go through Itteringham, still on narrow lanes, and turn **left** a

Gentle hills and rolling accents make rural Norfolk a charm for cycling. (Bill North)

couple of miles later ("Saxthorpe, Norwich, Mannington") and then immediately **right** ("Plumstead, Holt"). Go through **Baconsthorpe** (27 miles) (there's a sign here for Baconsthorpe Castle) and follow signs to **HOLT** (30 miles).

Turn **left** in the town onto the **A148** ("King's Lynn, town centre") and go immediately **right** ("town centre"). Go **left** at the war memorial into the center of town and then **right** opposite the King's Head pub at the other end of the main street ("Cley next the sea"). It's pronounced *Klye,* by the way.

If you get as far as the junction with the A148 again, you've gone one turn too far for the road to Cley.

Continue along the **Cley road** for a couple of miles and look for signs to Blakeney. Follow those signs to **Blakeney** (36 miles). Go across the **main road** ("Blakeney quay") and enjoy a cup of coffee in a quaint waterside village. Be warned, though: it can be busy on warm days.

The biggest attraction of Blakeney, apart from its waterfront, are the trips out to see seals basking on outlying spits of sand and shingle. Two operators run small boats leaving according to the tide (Blakeney is now almost landlocked as the sea recedes and even shallow vessels have difficulty making it in and out of the creek). The sailors are John Bean (0263-740038) and Jim Temple (0263-740791).

The outlying marshes and nearby Scolt Island are bird reserves and the whole area is a temple for ornithologists, who flock here all year when their telephone network spreads word of a rare bird blown ashore during migration.

Holkham Hall, about 10 miles farther along the coast from Blakeney, is the home of the Coke family (pronounced Cook). It was the birthplace of many important agricultural reforms as well as being a magnificent old pile in its own right. Coke's farm pioneering was celebrated by his tenants, who collected £4,000 in 1845 (then a vast sum for anyone, let alone peasant farmers) to build a 120-foot column in his memory.

The house is privately owned, but it's open to visitors. The grounds were laid out by Capability Brown in 1762. The art collection includes Rubens, Vandyke, Claude Poussin and Gainsborough. There's also a deer park with a lake. It's basically open from Easter to fall, but the pattern isn't straightforward (0328-710227).

Twenty miles farther round the coast is **Heacham,** where the village sign portrays a Red Indian princess called Pocahontas. She married a local man in 1614 and, although she died at 22, she had a son. The boy moved to Virginia and began a family which eventually gave birth to Woodrow Wilson.

After Blakeney, retrace to the **main road** and turn **right** on the **A149** (King's Lynn). There are signs around here for the lobsters and crabs which are a feature of this North Norfolk coast.

Go down a gentle hill and then turn **left** on the **B1388** ("Walsingham"). In fact, if you ride on a circuit of Blakeney village, you'll emerge on the A149 opposite this turning.

You now start climbing again for a couple of miles, up away from the coast. It's not an arduous ride, so take your time. At the top is a turning to **Stiffkey** (some people say *Stewky*). Near Stiffkey, the **Cockthorpe Hall** toy museum—seven rooms in a 16th-century hall—has more than 3,000 toys. It's open daily except the Christmas holiday (0328-830293).

Stiffkey was also the home of a curious clergyman called Harold Davidson, who fell from grace and was defrocked in the 1930s after his well-meaning attentions to wayward ladies were misinterpreted in a less liberal era; he was subsequently mauled to death by a lion in a circus act in Skegness, on the Lincolnshire coast, and his body's now in Stiffkey churchyard. It was quite a thing at the time.

Anyway, back to the route . . . Go straight on, following signs for Walsingham, through **Langham** (38 miles). There's a barn in Langham in which you can see experts blowing and shaping articles in glass. It's open weekdays all year and weekends from May to September (0328-830511). There are brown tourist signs from the village.

Continue through **Binham** (40 miles), with a sign for Binham Priory. This was once a center for Benedictine monks, and the priory was built about 1100 as a kind of extension of the abbey in St. Albans (which is miles away in Hertfordshire, north of London, but that's monks for you). The abbey's no longer complete and part of it is now built into the village church, but it's worth a visit if you like architecture or religious history.

Be careful to turn **right** on the way out of the village. It's still signposted for Walsingham, but it's easily missed.

You reach **Great Walsingham** at 43 miles, but the attraction is the neighboring village of **Little Walsingham**. You'll find it farther down the same road.

There's a **T-junction** at the bottom. Turn **right** on the **Wells and Fakenham road (B1388)** if you want to get to the Slipper Chapel, a Roman Catholic shrine, and the other features of the village.

The Slipper Chapel has a charming story. In 1061, Lady Richeld (the name varies according to whose account you hear) had a vision. She was told to build a copy of the building in Nazareth in which the angel Gabriel told the Virgin Mary she was to have a child. She did as she was told, but not without difficulty.

The vision said she'd find a dry patch in a damp field and she should build there. She got it wrong, though, and the building kept falling down until she moved it. When the original wooden memorial stayed put, a stone church was added to it.

When word got about that the Virgin Mary's spirit had despaired of infidels in the Holy Land and moved to Norfolk, the low and the mighty began walking to Walsingham, stopping at shrines on the way. When they reached what is now the Slipper Chapel, they discarded their shoes and walked the last mile without them.

Before long, the shrine became very rich. Its visitors included Henry III and Edward I. That upset Cromwell, of course, and he came along and knocked everything down. Although the cult was revived at the end of the last century and a new shrine built just before World War II, not much of the original buildings and nothing of the first shrine survives.

It's still an important Roman Catholic center and candles burn in the church where prayers have been said and miracles celebrated. The village is lovely, if overburdened with souvenir shops, with Elizabethan houses, a cobbled square and lots of alleyways.

There are guided tours of Walsingham from the tourist center (0328-820250). There's also a music festival of mainly religious works in August (0328-820399). The British love for steam railroads is also catered to in Walsingham. A 10-inch-gauge railroad runs from Walsingham to Wells daily from Easter to the end of September.

Walsingham to King's Lynn: 39 Miles

Having visited the village, **retrace** to the **T-junction** where you came in and this time go straight on the **Great Snoring and Thursford road.**

Go through the wonderfully named village of **Great Snoring** (46 miles) (the local paper, making the most of another oddly named local village once had the headline "Seething Woman Kills Snoring Man"). Turn **right** at the village sign ("Fakenham"). You meet the **A148** again and go straight across ("Fakenham, Norwich") on to the **A1067.** That takes you to the center of **FAKENHAM** (50 miles).

There's a flea market in Fakenham—at the Old Cattle Market—on Thursday mornings. There's also, curiously, a museum dedicated to the making of gas and its use in, among other things, lamps and lighting. It's billed, enticingly, as the only complete gasworks in England and Wales. It's open periodically from spring to fall (0328-851696).

Follow the road right through the town and leave on the **Swaffham** (say *Swoff'm*) **and Wells road.** Before long you'll come to a **roundabout.** Turn **left** on the **A1065** ("Swaffham, East Dereham") and later **right** ("Helhoughton") (53 miles). Follow that through **Helhoughton** (56 miles). The road takes you round the side of West Raynham airfield. Go straight on along the road as indicated and then turn **left** at a **T-junction** (58 miles) ½ mile from the airfield ("Massingham"). Follow that sharply round to the right by the entrance to the airfield and then pick up signs for Harpley where the road divides (59 miles).

Go on, taking care to follow signs for Harpley. A mile later there's a **crossroads** where the road marking takes you to the left, but in fact you want to go straight (unsignposted) to **Harpley** (62 miles). Go straight on at the **junction** with the **A148,** where you cross over ("Houghton"). The moment you've crossed the main road, the lane splits. The direct route lies to the left. But if you take a 1-mile diversion to the right instead, it'll bring you to Houghton Hall, an 18th-century Palladian mansion built by Sir Robert Walpole. For some eccentric aristocratic reason, it has (and will show you) a collection of 20,000 model soldiers. The house and gardens is open three days a week from Easter to the end of September (East Rudham 569).

Your direct route, though, goes left at that fork. That brings you to a **T-junction.** The road straight ahead is just a **stony lane** of ¼ mile, but you can ride that way if you wish and save ½ mile or so. Alternatively, you can go **right** and then **first left** ("Bircham, Anmer") and come back to the end of the stony lane.

Either way, you'll eventually reach the **B1153** (85 miles). Cross over ("Anmer") into the immaculate village of **Anmer** (66 miles). By now, you'll have noticed how many villages in this part of Britain have beautiful wooden signs to name them, carved from wood and then painted. Most of them are the work of one man: Harry Carter.

Harry Carter was a teacher with a strong interest in local history and, conveniently, skilled at wood-carving. In the 1950s, villages in this part of Norfolk—with its strong royal connections—wanted to commemorate the coronation of Queen Elizabeth II. Harry made his first sign in this area and the idea caught on: Harry spent years and years making more and more signs.

There's one in Anmer, one side depicting an old-style, life-sized Boy Scout (a gift from local Scouts to the Queen) and the other a Roman centurion (marking Anmer's history).

The meticulousness of the villages and the occasional royal crests above shops and companies (a mark of royal patronage) are signs of how the villages around here are strongly influenced and possibly even belong to the Queen's private estate at **Sandringham,** to which this lane brings you (69 miles).

The first point of Sandringham you pass is the horse stud on the right with its statue of a horse. When you reach the **T-junction** beyond the stud, the wall ahead is that of the Sandringham estate, the Queen's private home. Sadly, the house—which is open to visitors during the summer—doesn't speak well of regal taste. One guidebook calls it "very ugly, like a huge and grandiose Victorian seaside hotel." Still, the Queen likes it.

Turn **right** by that wall (unsignposted) and take the first turn **left,** following the wall around the estate. The entrance to the house is on the left, just down this road. It's a big attraction and the road can get very busy. It is, though, a good lane with broad grass verges, often used for parking and picnicking.

Bircham windmill, 6 miles from Sandringham, still turns on windy

A place to call home: the Queen's private residence in Sandringham, Norfolk, is open to visitors.

days. It's again become both a working mill and a bakery. It's open daily except Saturday from late May to the end of September (048523-393). It's a pleasant ride if it's not too busy, through ferns and woods. In the end (71 miles) it'll bring you to the **A149.** Turn **left** and then **right** to **Wolferton** (72 miles). You can ride round Wolferton in a loop. The best way is to go **right** at the **first junction** (marked "M" for museum), ride through trees down to the village and then follow the road counterclockwise through this hamlet with royal connections.

It was here that the royal family used to disembark from the train that had brought them from London. They would then rest a little at the station before taking a carriage up the hill and across the main road to Sandringham. As with so much in Britain, neither the tracks nor the trains exist any longer, but part of the station has been turned into a museum of curious royal and railroad artifacts, displayed with gentle humor. Exhibits include Queen Victoria's traveling bed and Prince Edward's blue and gold lavatory.

It's odd to think that most of the kings and queens of Europe came to this tiny station over the decades. And so did Rasputin, the crazy Russian monk, but he was out on the next train back to town.

The museum's open daily over Easter and from April to September (0485-540674).

Go on through the village and back in the direction you came, **returning** to the **"M" junction** you passed on the way in. When you get to that junction, turn **right** (unsignposted) so that you're not riding back on the road you used on the way in.

That'll take you to the **main road.** Go straight over (unsignposted) to re-enter the ferns and woods of the Sandringham estate. After a while you reach the **B1439;** turn **left** (unsignposted, although you'll see the village sign of **West Newton**) (74 miles).

Don't go into the village. Instead, take the **first lane right,** next to the decorative West Newton sign. Continue through woods to the **A148** (76 miles). Turn **right** (unsignposted). The main road goes gently uphill. Toward the top is the first lane to the **right** (unsignposted). Take that **lane,** back through the trees, to the **A149.** Cross over ("Castle Rising") and go into **Castle Rising** itself (79 miles). The castle is on your left, built in the 12th century. Bizarrely, William the Conqueror gave it to his brother-in-law, a chap called Odo, then changed his mind and gave it to his butler instead, along with another castle at Old Buckenham, near Norwich. One obviously tipped the servants rather better in those days.

Castle Rising is an unspoiled village made of local materials, and even the one or two modern houses are well matched. By the church is the Howard Hospital, now an almshouse for old ladies. Every Sunday, they walk to church wearing pointed hats and red cloaks carrying the badge of the Howard family, their patron.

Follow signs for the village as far as the **T-junction.** Turn **left** and that **road** takes you all the way through **South Wootton** to the center of **King's Lynn** (82 miles).

If time's a bit short, you can take the train from here to London (if it's only middling-short, break the journey at Ely and then again at Cambridge, which are both on this line; Cambridge is world-famous, anyway, but Ely's worth seeing for its magnificent cathedral).

But have a look round King's Lynn before you leave. The outskirts are dreary and the shopping center's unsympathetic. But the market squares are splendid, with guildhalls and grand unspoiled houses and hotels. There's a high-class music festival here every July.

The waterside area is a small working port. A small ferry crosses the river to the much smaller village of West Lynn. There's not much to see on the other side, but the crossing gives you a panoramic view of the town. You can take a bike on the ferry, by the way.

Southwest of King's Lynn is the spectacular moated house of Oxburgh Hall, where the sky reflects in the water and games of croquet are still played on the lawns. It was built in 1482 and although the outside's been changed a bit since, it still looks much as it did 500 years back. It's in the village of Oxburgh itself. It belongs to the National Trust, which opens it from spring to fall, several days a week (036621-258).

King's Lynn to Norwich: 53 Miles

Leave King's Lynn on the **A1076** and **B1145,** which you'll have passed in the northern outskirts of the town. They're signposted to Gayton. You'll go through **Ashwicken** (86 miles) and enter **Gayton** (88 miles). Turn **right** on the **B1153** in the center ("Narborough"), through **East Walton** (90 miles) and then turn **left** shortly after the village. The road swings right and you go straight on, signposted Castle Acre and West Acre.

Follow signs for **West Acre** (93 miles). It's only a tiny place and not with much to commend it. Go down through the village and turn **left** to the sweeping bend of **South Acre** (95 miles). Then turn **left** down an **unsignposted lane,** across a ford which comes in the back way of **Castle Acre** (96 miles).

The village is named after the remains of its Norman castle, but there's also a ruined priory and a lovely church. It's a pretty village with winding streets and attractive old houses.

Leave again on the **road** to Sporle and Little Dunham, being sure to take the **left-hand road** where the lanes split soon after leaving the village. The Sporle and Dunham lane is narrow and rises gently, with hedges on both sides, and brings you (97 miles) to the unsignposted **junction** with the **A1065.** Go straight ahead ("Sporle") and follow signs for Sporle until, at 99 miles, there's a sign to the **left** for Little Dunham.

Take that **lane** into **Little Dunham** (101 miles), where you turn **right** in front of the Black Swan into an **unsignposted road.** Then turn **right** again at the end of that road, 1/2 mile later. That brings you 1/2 mile later to the **A47,** where you go **right** and then immediately **left** ("Necton"). Go down through the scruffy village of Necton and then at a bizarre-looking church and the village post office, turn left ("Bradenham") into **School Road.**

Now follow signposts to Bradenham. The signs might say Bradenham, West Bradenham or even East Bradenham, but the neighboring communities have now grown into each other, so that they're the same place.

When the signs for **Bradenham** end (106 miles), it's because you've arrived on the edge of the village, although there's no sign to tell you so. Go **right** and **left** at the **junction** and ride into the village.

The road takes you past the cricket ground, where you turn **left** to **Shipdham** (108 miles). Go **left** on the **A1075** ("East Dereham") through Shipdham. The road snakes round the impressive church. Immediately you've passed it, turn **right** ("Cranworth"). That turn is easy to miss, so take care.

Then comes **Cranworth** (111 miles), without a lot to say for itself, and then the hamlet of **Wood Rising** (112 miles). There's hardly anything there. Turn **left** at the end of what there is to **Hingham.** You get to the village outskirts at a **junction** with the **B1108** (115 miles). Turn **left** ("Barford, Norwich") and go into **Hingham.**

There are strong American connections here, because it was from Hingham that Robert Peck set off early in the 17th century to set up Hingham in Massachusetts. He'd been denied religious freedom and wanted to find it in America. A chap called Samuel Lincoln joined him in 1637 and from his family came one Abraham Lincoln. There's a small memorial in the impressive church to mark the links.

The best bits of Hingham are the parts you see first. There are some attractive old houses dotted around the church and then a short central road which seems surprisingly wide for such a small village. The far end of the village, though, is spoilt by a hodgepodge of modern housing and industrial buildings.

Ride through the village, ignoring the eyesores, and look for signs a couple of miles later for Wicklewood and Wymondham (say *Wind'm*). Turn **right** and follow signs to the center of **Wymondham** (121 miles).

Along this road is a sign urging you to "drive you steady, bor." The "bor" isn't a misprint for "boy"; it's the local shortening of the word neighbor, a term of greeting. The village of Kimberley is also signposted to the left. It's a collection of pretty houses and cottages edging a small green that stands beside a minor junction. Kimberley is an estate village, owned or at least initiated by the local aristocracy, who live in some seclusion in a grand house up a long, leafy but private path.

Ride to the edge of central Wymondham and then turn **right** to the spectacular old abbey, which you'll have seen on the ride toward the town. It was from here that monks used to run the town, not always that benevolently. Years ago, there was a huge row between the monks and the townspeople over whose bells should ring from the tower. To cut a long story, the monks ended up blocking up the center of the church so that the townsfolk could no long see the high altar.

When the monks then built a tower for their own bells, the town rioted and began building what was to have been an even bigger belltower at the other end of the abbey. By the time they got to 142 feet, they either lost interest or made friends with the monks, and so both towers have spent the remaining centuries looking somehow unfinished. The inside is well worth a visit.

Farther through Wymondham, to the top of the gentle climb through the town, is a timbered market house on stilts, built in 1617 with a conical roof. For many years markets were held beneath it (the surrounding area is now a parking lot, although there's still a small weekly market) and town council meetings were held in the room upstairs.

Over the years, though, the building became shabby and rickety and the councillors moved elsewhere. The house, now restored, houses the tourist information office.

Ride up to the market house and turn **right** just before it, so that it passes on your left. Ride to the end of that road and it brings you out, opposite a police station, into a **road** that crosses the main **A11** at traffic lights. Go across the A11 ("Bungay") into the **B1135** and ride down the hill past the access road to the railway station.

The station at Wymondham is unusual in that it's privately owned.

Village greens are the essence of old England's charm, although not every community has one. (Bill North)

It's become a sort of museum; it also serves meals and cream teas and sells pianos, a truly eccentric British combination.

British Rail closed it, as it closed so many minor stations. But a man called David Turner bought it and the railroad obliged by stopping trains there again (0953-606433).

Go under the railroad bridge and then turn immediately **left** (unsignposted) into **Rightup Lane.** That rises and then turns by some small industrial buildings. Continue along that lane, which will eventually be crossed by a new Wymondham bypass. Go across the **bypass,** ignore the one lane that runs to the right, and continue to the very end of the road, 1¹/₂ miles later.

At that **junction** (124 miles), turn **left** ("Hethel, Wreningham"). Go a few hundred yards and then turn **left** again ("Hethel"). That takes you ¹/₂ mile, up and over a bridge which once crossed rail tracks, to a **T-junction.**

Signposted to the right here is Lotus Cars, the surprisingly small Lotus sports car factory. Lotus, for many years an independent builder, is now part of General Motors. It produces some of the fastest sports cars in the world. A sign at the entrance also celebrates the world motor racing championships that the firm has won. The fenced-off area beyond the factory is an airfield where cars are tested beyond prying eyes, and the race cars are assembled and developed in an old manor house on the far side.

Unless you're a motor sports enthusiast, ignore the Lotus sign and turn **left** (unsignposted) instead. This takes you momentarily back toward Wymondham, gently downhill past some oil storage tanks. Freewheel for a few moments after the oil depot and then take the **first lane right** ("Ketteringham, East Carleton"), which is a pleasant if unexciting ride through fields and past trees to **Ketteringham.**

Go through the village. At the far end is a **junction** with a war memorial at its center. Go straight across ("Norwich, Cringleford"), under the railroad and across the Norwich southern bypass, and into **Cringleford** (132 miles). There's not a lot to commend this stretch of the village, but the end of the road brings you to just a few yards of the **A11,** the main London-to-Norwich highway. At this point the road itself has been bypassed, so that the heavy traffic is a few yards farther on and you have the old road instead.

Turn **right** on the old **A11** ("Norwich") and ride downhill into the older part of Cringleford. At the traffic lights, turn **left** into **Blue Bell Road,** under the new A11, and then turn **right** ("City Centre"), up on to the **A11** again. In other words, you've gone from the right to the left of the main road into Norwich, so that you end up on the proper side of the road.

Note that in Blue Bell Road there are signs for the Norwich cycle route, but the A11 becomes a lot quieter at its Blue Bell Road junction and there is a marked cycle lane for much of the route into Norwich. The choice is yours, but the A11 is the most direct and certainly the more obvious route.

It is, in any case, only 2 miles from this point into **NORWICH** (135 miles). Ride straight to the center. Your starting point, from the station, is then just ½ mile away.

But before you take the train, don't miss the chance to look around. There are two excellent ways of doing this. The first is to walk or cycle, of course. The other is to take a boat ride along the river and out to the Broads, an extensive system of ancient flooded peat quarries now much used by yachts and motorboats.

There's a tourist information center just higher up the hill from the multicolored awnings of the city center outdoor market. From there you'll get the times of the boat rides, which leave from Elm Hill quay and Foundry Bridge quay (0603-501220).

The signs as you enter Norwich call it "a fine city," and they're right. The architecture writer Nikolas Pevsner said "Norwich has everything," and he was right, too. There's a glorious cathedral with a needle-fine spire that's the second-highest in Britain (Salisbury has the tallest) and the body of Edith Cavell, the World War I nursing pioneer and martyr, rests in the graveyard; there are old timbered houses and cobbled streets, like Elm Hill and Tombland; there's a sturdy, square castle on its own hill; there are the remains of the city walls, and much, much more. Above all, the whole extensive center has the relaxed and confident air of a prosperous, historical and unspoiled provincial center—well worth a long look round.

TOUR NO. 17

THE GLORY OF MIDDLE ENGLAND
Warwickshire, Oxfordshire and Gloucestershire

Distance:	188 miles
Estimated time:	4 riding days
Terrain:	Usually gentle, but with a few short climbs
Maps:	Ordnance Survey 150, 151, 163, 164
Rail:	Warwick, from London (Euston), although it might be quicker to get off at Leamington Spa, 2 miles away— that could save a change of trains; there is a rail service to Stratford-upon-Avon from Birmingham

The spine of England varies dramatically. The north is the Pennine hills, even mountains, which form the country's backbone. South of Sheffield, though, are the industrial midlands and, below them, a strand of country which contains half the nation's gems.

There's Stratford with its Shakespeare connections, the castles of Warwick and Leamington, the startling palace at Blenheim, where Winston Churchill was born (and his grave, a few miles away), the colleges of Oxford, the picture-book villages of Lower Slaughter and Broadway, the gentle Vale of Evesham. This ride takes you to them all, and more besides.

When I came to plan where I would ride, I kept finding somewhere else that I wanted to see, 10 miles farther on. What started as daily excursions has grown to a tour of several days, and I don't regret it a moment. If you don't go on any of the other rides, you really should go on this one.

The way I've divided the tour isn't supposed to suggest they're daily quotas; they're just digestible chunks for the route. It's also possible to join and leave the route at many points by train, or to cut across country to make the loop shorter. Since these variations are virtually too many to mention, I've not mentioned them; if I had, another forest would have fallen to provide the paper.

Warwick to Woodstock: 58 Miles

Warwick Castle's magnificent, with an imposing and towered entrance to the stately buildings. Sir Walter Scott called it the most

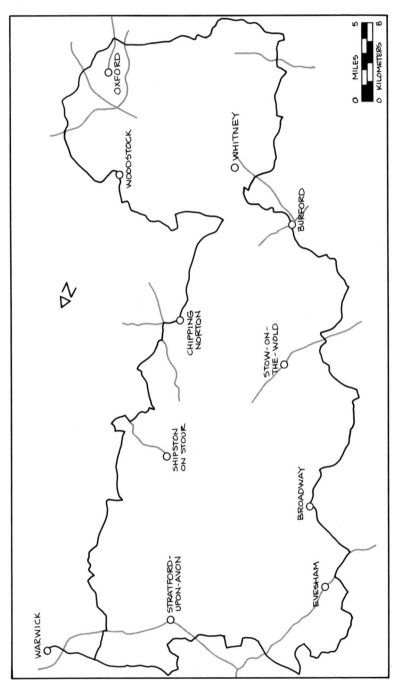

Warwick Castle, everyone's dream of what a castle should look like.

noble sight in England. Apart from the building, the most striking point is the 1,000 pieces of armor. It's open daily except Christmas (0926-495421).

In Warwick Church there's a chapel in memory of the Earl of Warwick, who was buried there after burning Joan of Arc. The man who made the stained glass windows took no shortcuts with the jewels in the illustrations—they're real.

Leave **Warwick** on the **B4095** toward Redditch and Henley. That'll take you out past the racecourse. A mile later, you're in the country. The road takes you over the **A46.** Skirt Hampton and then turn **left** ("Sherborne, Barford"). Cross the motorway to reach the A46. What you need is the road on the far side, but you can't go across. Instead, you have to go **left** on the **A46,** ride round the **roundabout** and then back down the other side, only then turning **left** into the **B4463,** Watery Lane ("Sherborne, Barford").

At the bottom of **Watery Lane** (5 miles) is a **T-junction.** Ten yards before it is a turn to the right, Fulbrook Lane. It's signposted Sherborne, but not clearly. Taking care not to turn right at the T-junction, turn **right** instead into Fulbrook Lane.

This is a pleasant, narrow lane with grassy verges. It's flat countryside, with grazing animals and calm fields. Keep going through the modern village of **Hampton Lucy** (8 miles), following signs to **Charlecote** (9 miles). Turn **right** on the **B4088** ("Wellesbourne, Stratford") and follow to **Wellesbourne.**

At this point, you can detour to **STRATFORD**—you can even pick up the far side of the tour there and go back to Warwick. But you'll come back to Stratford on the return trip in about 150 miles.

You get to the bypass before you reach Wellesbourne (10 miles). Turn **right** (A429, "Charlecote, Stratford, Stowe"). **Two roundabouts** follow within a few hundred yards. Then turn **right** and immediately **right** ("Walton") into another **grassy lane** to **Walton** (13 miles).

Two miles beyond it is a **crossroads.** Go straight over ("Pillerton") and then **right at a fork** soon afterward to **Pillerton Priors** (17 miles). Turn **right** in the village on the **B4451** ("Halford, Stow"), then **right** just afterward on the **A422** ("Stratford, Halford, Stow"), and then **left** on the **B4451** ("Halford, Stow") and then **left** again after 50 yards into an **unsignposted road.**

This is a road wide enough for just one car, with views of the vale on both sides. The road drops into the plain and brings you to a **crossroads** on the outskirts of **Fullready.** Turn **left** there ("Whatcote, Oxhill, Tysoe") and follow to **Whatcote** (20 miles).

Turn **right** in the village opposite the Royal Oak into a **lane** signposted to Brailes. Go on to a **crossroads** 1 mile later, and turn **left** ("Tysoe"). Carry on to the **first junction** and turn almost back on yourself to the **right** on an unsignposted, **more major road.** That takes you up the hill. At the top the road swings right but we go straight on ("Compton Wynyates, Epwell, Banbury"). The hill to your left is Windmill Hill and the mill stands with its sails intact. You'll have to look carefully, though, because trees hide it in summer.

It's part of the Compton Wynyates estate. Just beyond the mill, where the road starts to steepen, is the entrance on the left to Compton Wynyates House and some strict warnings to keep out. The house is only occasionally open, which is a shame because it's beautiful.

Take the first turn **right** (24 miles) ("Winderton, unsuitable for heavy vehicles") down into **Winderton** (25 miles). Turn **left** in the village ("Brailes") down the hill past Underhill Farm. There are some lovely honey-colored buildings here reminding you that we're approaching the Cotswolds. The village is pretty, if spoiled by a corrugated iron barn.

The land is now hillier, not badly so, but it'll have you going up and down the gears.

Go through **Lower Brailes** (26 miles), then **right** on the **B4035** ("Shipston"), through to the other side of the village and then **left** into **Sutton Lane** to the pretty stone village of **Sutton-under-Brailes** (28 miles).

Turn **left** ("Stourton, Cherington, Whichford, Morton") before the green by a fantastically shaped tree to **Stourton** (28 miles) and follow signs for **Whichford** (30 miles), taking care with the signs in Stourton.

Go through Whichford, a nice mixture of old and new stone, leaving on the **Hook Norton road.** That takes you up a steepish hill for 1 mile or so going southeast. At the top is a **T-junction** (31 miles) alongside a transmitter. Turn **right** to **Great Rollright** (where the church has a bizarre carving of a man being swallowed by a crocodile), and then in the village (33 miles) **right** again to the **Rollright Stones.**

The stones lie on the far side of the A3400, to the right of your road. You'll have to get off your bike and cross the hedge to see them. Historians say they're third in importance to Stonehenge and Avebury, although they're less striking. On the other side are a burial chamber and more prehistoric stones. Together, they were used for funeral ceremonies before 1500 B.C. That's what historians say, anyway.

Locally, legend says a local king was promised that if he could stand in the field and see nearby Long Compton, he'd be the king of all England (don't ask me why; the legend doesn't explain that). Normally this wouldn't have been a problem, but when the king climbed the hill he found that the witch who'd made the promise had conjured up a mist. The witch cackled, conjured up some magic, and turned the king and his followers into stone. To this day the lumps of old rock are called the King's Stone, the King's Men and the Whispering Knights.

There are good views to the right and, occasionally, open-air theater in fields to the left.

Pass the stones and take the first turn **left** ("Little Rollright, Chipping Norton") (35 miles) and go down a swooping hill, following signs through **Over Norton** to **CHIPPING NORTON** (38 miles). This is green, sweeping countryside, mainly arable and restful.

Chipping is an old word for market and the town was making a good profit 700 years ago. It's an airy town, with splendid stone buildings. Go into the center, over a double set of miniature **roundabouts,** taking care because they baffle everybody. Go through the town, following signs for Burford and Charlbury, leaving town on the **A361.**

Keep following signs for Burford A361 and you'll leave on **Burford Road.** Ignore the sign for Charlbury—we are going to Charlbury but we're going a longer and prettier way.

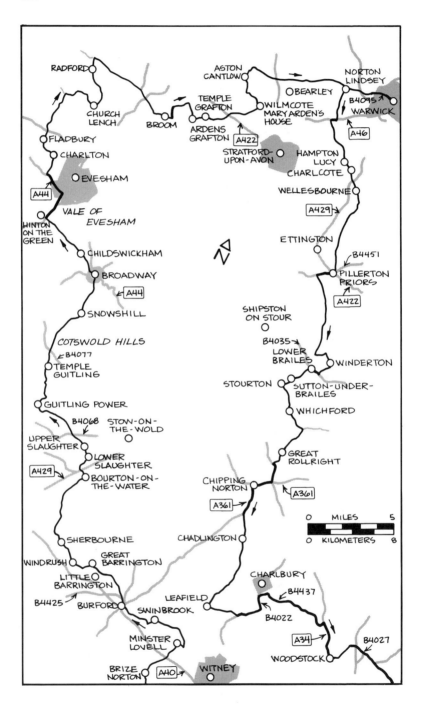

Go over the first minor **junction** and then, at 40 miles, turn **left** to **Chadlington** (42 miles). Go **left** and **right** in the village along **Horse Shoe Lane** to **Leafield.**

That takes you round the edge of Wychwood Forest, between which and Charlbury is Cornbury deer park. There are paths through the wood which connect the two. It's owned by the National Trust and there is, presumably, one fewer deer than there might have been; word has it that Shakespeare was arrested for poaching here. The house in the middle is still occupied, but it's open five days a week from the start of April to the end of October (0789-470277).

This is a wooded lane, very pleasant for several miles.

In **Leafield** (47 miles), turn **left** in and out of the woods to **Charlbury** (51 miles). Due south of here—by going straight on at Leafield—is the blanket-making town of Witney. Blankets are made in factories, which blend in as well as factories are ever likely to blend, but the rest of the town has its quaint and even attractive parts.

Charlbury is a disappointment. On the outskirts, turn **right** ("Woodstock"). The road runs east to the **junction** with the **A34**. Just before the junction, on the right, is Ditchley Gate, the rear entrance to Blenheim Palace.

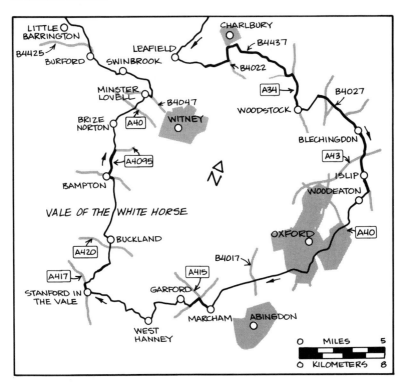

Blenheim is where Winston Churchill was born. John Churchill was the first Duke of Marlborough and Queen Anne gave him the money to put up this breathtaking old house because he won the Battle of Blenheim in 1704. There's a Churchill exhibition, which includes the room in which he was born. Capability Brown designed the grounds, which go on forever (2,100 acres). The palace and grounds are open daily from mid-March to the end of October (0993-811325).

Just south of Blenheim is Bladon, with quaint cottages, a pump and the Old Malthouse. It is here that Winston Churchill was buried in January 1965. He lies in the churchyard with his mother, Lady Randolph, who was the daughter of an American newspaper tycoon. The house in which he spent his last years, by the way, is a feature of the Garden of England tour.

Turn **right** on the **A34** (formerly A44) into **WOODSTOCK** (58 miles) and you'll find the entrance signposted on the right. This is a busy road and a busy town, but there's no other way. The stone wall to the right is the boundary of Capability Brown's park.

Woodstock is striking and intriguing but dedicated to tourists. It maintains a certain classiness, though, not least in its number of hotels—the Bear Inn was built in 1237—and restaurants, making it an oasis for coffee and cakes. Look out for the wonderful chimneys.

Woodstock to Burford: 57 Miles

You now have a choice. You can save a few miles by going straight on to Oxford. But be warned. The road, while direct, is busy and unpleasant. It becomes a dual carriageway just beyond the town and carries much of the traffic from the north into the city of Oxford.

To avoid that, turn **left** in Woodstock on the **road** signposted for Tackley. It's a narrow turn in the center. After a few hundred yards, take care to take **Banbury Road** to the **left,** still signposted Tackley. If you go past a small bike shop on your left, you've gone too far.

Follow the Tackley road to the **junction** with the **B4027** 1 mile later and turn **right** ("Tackley, Banbury, Wheatley") to **Bletchingdon** (63 miles).

Turn **right** by the green to **Hampton Poyle** (65 miles), and go on to the A43. This is a busy road, but there's a wide edge which makes cycling safer. You have to take it because you can't go straight across, as you once used to, to Islip.

So, turn **left** on the **A43** ("Northampton, Bicester, Brackley") and follow it to the **flyover junction** 1 mile later. Then turn **left** and **left again** for **Islip** (68 miles), on the edge of Ot Moor. St. Edward the Confessor was born here in 1004 and a portrait of him in the church quotes from his will: "I have given to Christ and St. Peter in Westminster ye little town of Islippe wherein I was born."

The village is quaint, with stone walls that close in on the road. It's where people move to when they've made their money working in Oxford.

Go straight through on the **B4027** for 1 mile, down a hill past the turn for Noke, then turn **right** to the attractive hamlet of **Woodeaton** (70 miles), with its willows, cottages and dumpy church. If you're feeling down on your luck, visit the church. There's a huge mural of St. Christopher, the traveler's friend. A 14th-century version of a bubble coming out of his mouth says, in French: "Whoever will see this image today will not die a violent death."

This lane now takes you directly to Oxford from the north and before long you'll see the tall buildings on the city outskirts. Oxford is bounded to the north by the busy A40. You need to take care to make sure you don't end up on it by mistake.

At the bottom of the lane from Woodeaton, you'll come to a **T-junction** (72 miles). Turn **right** and follow signs for Marston, over the A40. You're now in the city outskirts. Go **left** and **right** into **Marston Road** at **double roundabouts** by a gas station in New Marston and follow signs for **OXFORD** city center (75 miles).

The route through the center takes you past many of Oxford's grandest buildings—"That sweet city with her dreaming spires," as Matthew Arnold put it.

You can tour Oxford and the colleges—only the Sorbonne in Paris is older—on a double-decker bus all year. There are also boat tours from Folly Bridge. There's so much to see that you need a guidebook.

To leave **OXFORD**, follow the road as it moves through the center and then swings left over the river. Follow the sign "All Routes" and you'll come out on the south on the **A4144.**

Eventually you'll meet the southern ring road at a **roundabout.** Turn **right** ("A34, the north, the west"). Go on to the next **roundabout** and take the **exit** signposted Boars Hill and Wotton, up Hinksey Hill.

Boars Hill was the site of one of the world's most puzzling murders. Two pensioners were found battered to death in a cottage locked from the inside. There were no clues. The police fingerprinted everyone in the village to no avail. Nobody was ever arrested. In the end they concluded the two old people had had an almighty row, thrown the crockery about and killed each other in the process.

Go into **Boars Hill** (79 miles) by bearing **right** ("Boars Hill, Wotton") and go onto the **B4017.** Turn **left** and immediately **right** into **Honeybottom Lane** to **Marcham** (84 miles). Turn **right** on the **A415** ("Witney"), then **left** on the **A338** ("Wantage") ³/₄ mile later.

Look out for a pub called The Ark, ¹/₂ mile after the **junction,** then take the **first lane to the right** to Garford. Go through **Garford** (87 miles) and then **left** 1¹/₂ miles later to **West Hanney** (89 miles). You now zigzag across country for a while, so . . .

Turn **right** in **West Hanney** ("Denchworth, Charney Bassett,

Goosey"). The road winds through high hedges with distant hills. After about 1 mile, take the **second lane right** ("Charney Bassett"), then **left** ("Goosey, Challow station"), then **first right** ("Park Lane") to the **junction** with the **A417.** Turn **right** there (unsignposted) to **Stanford in the Vale.** This is the Vale of the White Horse.

In **Stanford** (94 miles), turn **right** ("Stanford village, Pusey, Buckland") through stone cottages with thatched and slate roofs; a good mix of old and new.

Leave by **Bow Road** and follow signs to **Buckland** (98 miles), crossing the **A420** to enter the village. Follow the road through the village, round the bend to the left and past the entrance to the grandeur of Buckland House, which is now a stone college of some substance. Then cross a humped-back bridge and turn **right** to Bampton. The road to Bampton is flat, through wheatfields, but watch out for the little river that you cross. It's the fledgling Thames, unrecognizable here from the broad river that flows through London. In these parts, it has the alternative name of Isis.

Go into **Bampton** (102 miles). It's a handsome village, all stone, but a lighter color than before. Go **right** on the **A4095** at the market square **roundabout** and follow signs through Brize Norton to Minster Lovell.

Brize Norton is best known now for its airbase. Unlike many places taken over by the military, the village center looks unaffected by the thousands of servicemen.

Go straight through and by going beneath the A40 you'll reach **Minster Lovell** (108 miles). Go **right** on the **B4047** ("Witney") and then immediately **left** opposite the White Hart ("Leafield"). You're now alongside the river Windrush, in whose valley we're going to stay for some miles.

Follow the road as it swings down on a tree-lined road, following the sign for Minster Lovell hall. At the bottom of the hill, go **left** over an old stone bridge, still signposted Leafield. On the right is one of the most attractive village cricket fields in the country.

It's a mistake to think that every Englishman is a cricketing fanatic, but many are and almost everyone has some understanding of the rules, which have an Old Colonial eccentricity. Village cricket is played faster than the international Test matches, and brawny-armed cowmen lash the ball into neighboring fields before being bowled out by the postman. Although it's mainly an opportunity to eat cucumber sandwiches, applaud politely and watch the sky for approaching rain (in which case everything stops), it would be a mistake to underestimate the religious fervor with which village cricketers play.

Good luck to you if you do see a game. Most spectators, hearing your accent, will be delighted to explain the rules—often embroidering their complexity for their amusement and your bewilderment. Do ask.

Pass the cricket field, go over a bridge and up the hill, then **fork**

left and follow signs to **Swinbrook.** You're heading for Burford and that won't take you into Swinbrook, but the village is worth a look. Some villages in the Cotswolds—the rolling, green-topped hills you're entering—have been tainted or spoiled by tourism. Swinbrook remains an unknown gem, though, an unassuming everyday village of crooked streets. You'll fall in love with it; it's the kind of village in which Agatha Christie's Miss Marple might bumble round the corner any moment.

Do have a look. When you have, re**turn** to the **T-junction,** cross the river and follow signs to **BURFORD** (115 miles).

BURFORD's attractive, a broad steep hill leading to a three-legged bridge across the Windrush and to the Cotswolds beyond. The stone buildings are warm and striking. It is, though, in every guidebook to Britain, which means every guidebook-buyer turns up. It's overconscious of its prettiness and its history. But then, who would blame it? It was here, after all, that the King of Mercia decided in 683 to have Easter at the same time as the rest of Christendom.

There are plenty of hotels and a few restaurants.

Burford to Evesham: 36 Miles

The pleasantest part of Burford isn't the main street but Sheep Street, which runs at 90 degrees to the main street, halfway down the hill. It's by **Sheep Street** that we leave the town, just below the war memorial, alongside the Tolsey museum—once where local wool barons gathered to trade.

Sheep Street is the **B4425.** The tourist information office is on your right, partway along. On the left, almost opposite, are the tiny editorial offices of *The Countryman,* a monthly magazine celebrating the British countryside.

Ride ½ mile from the center, clearing the buildings, and then turn **right** into an **unsignposted lane**—the first lane on the right. This narrow road is in Upton, although again it isn't signposted.

This charming lane follows the Windrush to your right. It's just wide enough for a single car, but there's rarely any traffic. The road dips and bobs and narrows; watch for puddles in the dips.

The lane take you to the attractive village of **Little Barrington** (118 miles) with its hilly green and stone cottages. Turn **right** at the **junction** and go downhill, but don't cross the river. Instead, just before the Fox Inn, turn **left** ("Windrush, Sherborne"). Go through **Windrush** and follow signs for **Sherborne** (111 miles).

Turn **right,** following signs for **Bourton-on-the-Water.** You can follow those signs all the way if you wish, but there's a better way 1 mile outside Bourton. There, the road splits and the sign points you to the left. The road **right** is marked "No PSVs except local buses." Take that **lane** and it'll bring you straight into **Bourton** (127 miles).

The glory of Blenheim Palace—Churchill grew up here, and he's buried in a nearby village.

All is not lost **if you go the other way.** You'll simply be led down to the main road, where you turn **right** and then **right again** a little later, following the main tourist signs.

Bourton is a tourist trap best visited outside peak season. Its appeal is the river beside the lawns of the main street. But there's also a stone model of the village behind the New Inn.

Leave Bourton by **Station Road** to the **junction** with the **A429.** Turn **right** ("Stow") and then **left** after ½ mile ("The Slaughters"). The attraction is **Lower Slaughter,** a wonderful, unspoiled hamlet in which the river runs down the main street.

Turn **left** alongside the river Eye, after the pub, following the sign for **Upper Slaughter,** which is to the right. It was here that the Reverend F. E. Witts wrote *Diary of a Country Parson.* His home's a hotel now, but otherwise little's changed; the last house built here was in 1904. There's a lovely manor house next to the hotel.

Follow the road past the Manor House, signposted Cheltenham. When you reach the **B4068,** turn **left** ("Cheltenham") and then follow signs to **Naunton**. The turn into the village is at the bottom of the hill. Anywhere else, it'd be a gem, but there are so many round here that they spoil you.

Follow through the village and climb back up the other side. At the top you'll get back to the **B4068.** You don't have to go quite as far as the B-road. At the **junction, turn back** on yourself ("Guiting Power, Winchcombe") to go back down the hill.

Go **right** at the **T-junction** ("Guiting Power, Winchcombe") and then at the gates of Guiting Grange go straight on along a broad, tree-lined lane to **Temple Guiting** (137 miles).

That'll bring you to the **B4077.** Turn **left** ("Tewkesbury"). About $3/4$ mile later comes the second lane on the right, at the top of a gentle hill immediately after a sign saying Cotswold Way Rough Collies. Turn **right** into that **lane** (unsignposted except for a warning of 7.5 tonne weight restriction).

The road's a fork away from the B-road, with trees on both sides. To your left is the long strip of Stanway Ash wood. In the gaps in the hedgerows and wild flowers to the right are the Cotswolds.

Along this road is a fork. It's straightforward—you go straight ahead—but if there's any doubt, the way you want is marked "unsuitable for motors." It's suitable for cycling, though, with grass down the middle. Finally, at the bottom of the hill, is the **left** turn to Snowshill and Broadway.

Snowshill (142 miles) is exceptionally pretty, with the manor belonging to the National Trust. From the outside it's just another big old house. Inside, though, is Charles Wade's remarkable collection of . . . well, everything, really. His coat of arms had the motto "Let nothing perish" and he took it literally. He collected so much, including a full-scale model of a Samurai dressed for battle, that by the time he died in 1956, he'd had to move into an outhouse to make room for it all. In all that time, he lived like a hermit, refusing to have electric light.

BROADWAY (145 miles), which lies beyond, is also pretty, but it's fallen prey to tourism. Not for nothing is it called the most publicized show village in England. It's not that the village, its flower-covered cottages, its grass verges and its old buildings have been spoiled— they haven't particularly (although there are the inevitable Old Gyfte Shoppes); it's just the spectacular numbers of people who come here.

High above Broadway to the southeast is Broadway Tower, 1,000 feet up. Its joy is that it's there solely because the builder wanted it there. It has no other purpose. It's 65 feet high and made of mellow brown stone, and the 6th Earl of Coventry put it there because he thought it looked good. It's surrounded by a commercial country park. From the top, on a good day, you're supposed to be able to see Warwick castle, Worcester cathedral and Tewkesbury abbey.

In Broadway, go **left** on the **A44** and then **left** again on the **B4362**

("Cheltenham, Winchcombe"). You'll also see signs for the restored Great Western Steam Railway, which is 5 miles southeast at Toddington.

From the **B4362,** go immediately **right** through **Childswickham** (146 miles) to **Hinton on the Green,** through flatter countryside signaling the start of the Vale of Evesham. At **Hinton** (150 miles), the **A435** takes you into **EVESHAM** (151 miles).

On the way, the dome-shaped hill to the left is Bredon Hill. The village of Bredon is worth a visit. The longest-running soap opera in the world is the early-evening serial on Radio 4, "The Archers." The fictional village of Ambridge, where the story evolves, is at the foot of Bredon Hill.

EVESHAM's pronounced *Eve-sh'm,* but the local accent puts in an extra syllable, so you get *Eva-sh'm.* Its charm is the tree-lined walks by the river, and some good old houses, but it's busy, a center of commerce. And like a lot of commercial capitals, it's been fought over. A mile due north, an obelisk marks the gruesome Battle of Evesham in August 1265. In a thunderstorm, Henry III's son put down local barons who'd developed ideas above their station. In the process, 160 knights and 4,000 soldier-peasants died in three hours.

Evesham to Stratford and Warwick: 37 Miles

Leave **Evesham**—which is twinned with Evesham, New Jersey, U.S.A.—on the **A44** ("Worcester, Evesham, Pershore") alongside the river Avon.

On the town outskirts, shortly after power cables, is the road **right** to **Charlton** (154 miles). For the sake of 1 mile, take a trip here to Cropthorne. There's a cedar that villagers say was planted before the Norman invasion of 1066. And northwest from here is a village with one of England's bizarrest names—Wyre Piddle (the Piddle Brook is a tributary of the Avon).

From Charlton, go on to **Fladbury** (which has a water mill, a Norman church and an old pub behind the landing stage) and cross the **B4084** by going **right** and **left** ("The Lenches, Bishampton").

You're now leaving the Vale of Evesham, although the apple and pear orchards continue for a few miles yet. Once the orchards covered endless acres and supplied most of what Britain needed, but times change.

Go up the hill, then turn **right** (unsignposted) into the **first lane.** Carry on climbing and pick up signs for **Church Lench** (160 miles), **Rous Lench** (162 miles—look out for half-timbered houses with ornate chimneys) and **Radford** (163 miles). Turn **right** in Radford ("Abbots Morton, Alcester").

The route doesn't go there, but Alcester—3 miles northeast—is the site of Ragley Hall, the stately home of the 8th Marquess of Hertford (a marquess, or marquis, is a form of lord). It's open from mid-April to the end of September (0789-762090).

The country is quieter now as Worcestershire gives way to Warwickshire. The riding is easy and the roads are dotted with crooked, half-timbered houses several hundred years old.

At **Weethley Gate** (167 miles), you reach the **A441.** Turn **right** ("Evesham") and then go straight over the **A435** Birmingham–Evesham road. Go across to **Dunnington** and **Broom** (169 miles).

Now you zigzag but essentially go straight ahead. At the end of the village, turn **left** at a **T-junction** into **Bidford Road** ("Wixford, Bidford, Alcester"), **right** on the **B4085** ("Bidford"), and then **left** into a **lane** following signs for **Ardens Grafton** (171 miles) and **Temple Grafton** (62 miles). Go straight through, down a one-in-nine hill, across a **staggered junction** at the Blue Boar, on to the **A422.**

If you turn **right** here, **STRATFORD-UPON-AVON** is 4 miles east. Alternatively, you can continue along the route and follow signs to Stratford from Wilmcote.

On the way, make a side trip to Binton. In St. Peter's church, the windows tell the tale of Captain Scott's expedition to the South Pole in 1912. That was the one on which Captain Oates walked out into the snow, saying "I may be a little while." The window says, "here, unwilling to be a burden to his companions leaves them and the shelter of the tent, to die." The rector was Scott's brother-in-law and Scott called in to say goodbye.

As for Stratford itself, well, you can find all you want from a thousand guidebooks. It's leafy, it's not totally spoiled, but it is crowded in high summer. It's a splendid place for meeting fellow travelers, who help make it the busiest English touring center outside London.

There are five buildings in and around the town connected with the old playwright. You can get details from the Shakespeare Birthplace Trust (0789-204016). In general, they're open all year except the Christmas holiday and, in some cases, on winter Sundays.

You can tour Stratford every day by double-decker bus. They leave the Pen and Parchment pub at Bridgefoot and visit all five Shakespeare buildings.

The Royal Shakespeare and Swan Theatre are in Waterside, near the town center beside the Avon. The Royal Shakespeare puts on five of Shakespeare's plays, and those of his contemporaries such as Marlowe and Johnson, each year. The other theater is for modern writers. You can take a guided tour backstage (0789-296655 for details, or 0789-295623 for the box office).

Continuing along the route . . . cross the **A422** ("Billesley") and then take the **first lane right** by the edge of Billesley Manor Hotel to **Wilmcote** (175 miles).

It's down a side street in the village that you'll find Mary Arden's House, home to Shakespeare's mother. It's a Tudor farmhouse, now more of a museum. Anne Hathaway's cottage is at Shottery, also signposted from here. It was there that Anne Hathaway lived before becoming Mrs. Shakespeare.

Continue through the otherwise undistinguished village of Wilmcote and follow signs for **Aston Cantlow** (177 miles), **Bearley** (180 miles), **Norton Lindsey** (184 miles), and from there you can follow the ornate signpost back to **WARWICK** (188 miles).

TOUR NO. 18

CHILTERNS AND THE VALE OF AYLESBURY

Buckinghamshire

Distance: 67 miles
Estimated time: 2 riding days
Terrain: Hilly at the beginning and end, but mostly moderate
Maps: Ordnance Survey 166, 165
Rail: Berkhamsted, about 30 minutes north of London (Euston)

This is a ride of constant beauty and charm through the soft and wooded downs of the northern Chiltern Hills and the Vale of Aylesbury, northwest of London. It starts in beech woods, passes through open undulating country, and ends in the Chiltern foothills.

It passes through the tranquil Ashridge Estate, followed by the picture-book village of Aldbury, with its ancient stocks (in which convicts were locked before being pelted with rotten fruit and worse) by the pond, and on past the grandeur of Mentmore and another Rothschild house, Waddesdon.

It finishes by skirting the prime minister's country house at Chequers and finishes with a view of the highest hill in the Chiltern range.

There's always something different, always something unusual.

Berkhamsted to Quainton: 32 Miles

Leave **BERKHAMSTED** station by White Hill, alongside what remains of the castle. It belongs to English Heritage, a fancy name for the Ministry of Works. The moat is still there, empty now, and parts of the walls and the castle mound. Apart from that, there's not a lot, and the best view is from farther round White Hill.

Skirt the castle and turn into **New Road,** keeping the castle on your left. This is a steady, gentle climb through sheep country. You're making your first entry into the Chilterns, a range of chalk hills which rise in Dorset (although they're not called the Chilterns there) and end in Cambridgeshire. It's only the section from the Thames to just beyond Berkhamsted that's commonly known as the Chilterns.

They never get above 900 feet but their edges can be steep. Their claustrophobic remoteness from the capital made them a home of rebellion (against the Romans, then against Charles I to start the Civil War, and then later as the founders of Quakerism) and of huge wealth, principally in the Rothschild family, which had six great mansions in the region.

You are also about to enter the 4,000 acres of the Ashridge Estate, owned by the National Trust. There are woods, roaming fallow, muntjak and Chinese water deer, and strange memorials to long-gone heroes.

Get to the top of the hill and you'll see the first of these memorials. It's to the Inns of Court Training Corps, who in this neighborhood trained more than 12,000 men to serve as commissioned officers in the "Great War." The Inns of Court are the center of English justice in London.

Turn **right** ("Potten End, Water End"), ride through Berkhamsted golf course and then take the first turn **left** ("Frithsden, Nettleden") and follow it through beech trees and bracken through **Nettleden** (3 miles) to **Little Gaddesden** (5 miles). And there you come across the second curious monument.

Little Gaddesden is a string of brick cottages with decorative chimneys. This is expensive commuter country. The buildings are separated from the road by a long green, and in the center is a tower. It looks like a war memorial, but it isn't. Around the base it reads "In memory of Adelaide, wife of Aidelbert, the 3rd Earl Brownlow . . . and daughter of Henry the 18th Earl of Shrewsbury and Talbot: Righteousness and peace have kissed each other, mercy and truth have met together."

Old Francis Henry, on the Gaddesden memorial, was a member of the Bridgewater family which pioneered canals in Britain. He left £8,000 to literary men who wrote religious essays.

Turn round from the monument and the big house through the trees in the valley is Ashridge College, the heart of the estate. It was built—or part of it, anyway—in 1276 as a College of Bonshommes. James Wyatt restored it in 1808 and it's now the Bonar Law College, named after an old prime minister. The College of Bonshommes was suppressed in 1575.

Across the hill in the other direction is **Great Gaddesden,** the home of the Halsey family for more than 450 years—usually at Gaddesden Place—and there are some interesting monuments to them in the Halsey chapel of the village church. The village is worth a diversion if you have time.

From Little Gaddesden, press on to the junction with the **B4506** at **Ringshall** (7 miles) and turn **left** ("Berkhamsted, Tring") alongside an eccentric building now used as a car dealership.

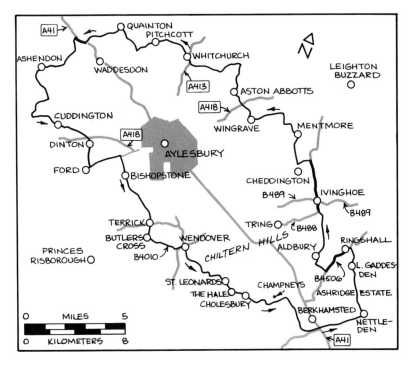

If you want a diversion, turn **right** at Ringshall and follow the signs to **Whipsnade** open-air zoo—one of the centers of European zoological research, as well as being open to the public. Its position is made clearer to passing jumbo jets by an enormous lion cut into the chalk hillside of the Dunstable Downs and edged at night by lights. There are more than 2,000 animals wandering mainly loose in fields.

From Ringshall, cross into Buckinghamshire and follow the road **left.** Immediately after the bend, you'll see a long, straight path to the **right.** It leads to a tall, slender monument to the Duke of Bridgewater, the father of inland navigation. It was put up in 1832, there are 172 steps to the viewing gallery, and you can see for miles across beautiful countryside. Many of the trees blew over in a gale in the late 1980s, but recovery has been rapid. The monument's open from April to October. There are also signposted bridleways, which you can explore by bike.

Return to the **B4506** and take the next turn **right,** to **Aldbury.** Take care on the descent. If you take it carefully, you'll enjoy views of Aldbury.

There's a tight bend at the bottom, followed by Galleon Cottage, which has a model sailing ship on its dovecote and chimney, and then the triangular village green and pond. The stocks, the whipping post, the church and the cottages reflected in the water have pushed up Kodak shares over the years. There are thatched cottages and 300-year-old almshouses saved for the poor of the village.

The route doesn't go this way, but were you to go straight on in Aldbury, you'd cross one of Bridgewater's prettiest canals and also the main railroad from London to Manchester. The cutting in which the tracks lie is the deepest in Britain and was dug at the cost of many lives by workmen brought mainly from Ireland (called "navvies" from their work on the navigation canals). They were so unruly that there were rumors of cannibalism and the Bishop of St. Albans sent missionaries to save their souls.

The station here is called Tring, but the town is 2 miles farther. The Rothschild family refused to let it run any nearer the town—where they owned the mansion and demolished a village and rerouted the main road to accommodate a collection of zebra and other exotic animals. The family collection of stuffed animals and birds is in a museum in Akeman Street. It includes the world's largest collection of dead fleas, including one dressed as a man, the other as a woman, in properly formed clothes.

The collection was built up by Lionel Rothschild. Shortly before World War II, it became part of the Natural History Museum, which has its main building in Kensington, west-London.

The town is 1,000 years old. In the parish church, in the town center, there's a monument to a female ancestor of George Washington.

After your pictures in Aldbury, turn **right** into **Stocks Road.** You now skirt the Ashridge estate and, after a couple more hills, you're into the Vale of Aylesbury. Just outside the village is Stocks Hotel. In the 1970s it belonged to an executive of the *Playboy* organization and tales abound of what is supposed to have happened there.

The road is narrow, climbing and then descending to the **B488**. Turn **right** ("Ivingoe, Dunstable, Leighton Buzzard") and look left (trying to ignore the cement works) for Pitstone windmill. It was built in 1627 but a gale in 1902 ended its working life. It was repaired in the 1960s and it's now open on summer Sunday afternoons. Ignore signs for Ivinghoe Beacon (800 feet high and once used for warning fires, hence its name), unless you want fine views and close-up glimpses of flying gliders, or to stand on the ancient Icknield Way.

The Icknield Way (also known locally as The Ridgeway) is the oldest road in Britain, probably older than the Bronze Age. It runs the length of the Chilterns and delighted the poet Robert Brooke, who said:

> *I'll take the road . . .*
> *The Roman road to Wendover*
> *To Tring and Lilley Hoo*
> *As a free man may do.*

Go on into **Ivinghoe** (14 miles), which gave its name to Walter Scott's *Ivanhoe*. The church has implements inside for pulling thatch off burning cottages. It's also got ancient funny faces carved into the designs of the medieval pews. The roof is spectacular with huge angels spreading their wings. Next door is the Georgian youth hostel, once a brewery. Across the road is the 15th-century King's Head and the rather newer Station Road.

Take **Station Road,** over the canal, and on to the turn to **Cheddington** (16 miles) and Mentmore. Turn **left,** over the railroad, and then **right** at the next **crossroads** to **Mentmore.**

If you go straight on instead of turning to Cheddington station, you'll see a turn which runs under the railroad at a brick bridge. Here—Bridego Bridge—is where one of the world's most audacious robberies took place in the early 1960s. Small-time villains held up a train carrying millions of pounds in used bills. One of the thieves, Ronnie Biggs, escaped jail and lives now in Brazil. Numerous attempts to bring him back have failed and he has become a folk anti-hero as a result.

The parkland you ride through after Cheddington once also belonged to the Rothschilds, who lived at Mentmore Towers, the big house you can just make out on the horizon, slightly to the left. Sadly, the family didn't take death taxes into account; in 1977, the house and its contents were sold for $15 million, then an unbelievable sum, to pay off the government. The house became a center for transcendental meditation.

Go up the hill, ignore the turn next to a pub, and go down the other side to a **crossroads.** Turn **left** to **Wingrave,** then **right** to **Aston Abbotts** (22 miles). Now's the time to get your camera ready for views across the Vale and to the distant Chilterns.

In Aston Abbotts, turn **left** at the green on to a road marked "Weedon, gated road." The road is public and the gates are usually open. Leave them how you find them and ride to **Weedon** (25 miles), a pretty village, enjoying the views and emerging eventually on to the **A413,** north of Aylesbury.

Turn right to **Whitchurch** (28 miles) and then, at the end of the village, left ("Oving, Pitchcott, North Marston"). Now follow signs to **Quainton,** enjoying the views.

There are signs of very early history soon after Pitchcott. Keep your eye open for seemingly random mounds of earth from prehistoric times. After **Quainton** (32 miles) is more recent history. When the London subway was built, one company, the Metropolitan, planned to extend the network far beyond London. The suburbs that developed became known as Metro-land and began the spread of London between the wars. The Metropolitan eventually met the main Great Central Railway at Quainton, although thankfully the suburbs didn't stretch as far. The line failed. Quainton station remains as a museum, with working steam trains offering public rides.

It's said that the people of Quainton have the strongest rural accents in Buckinghamshire. Quainton is one of the prettiest villages for miles, with a green, a pond, old cottages and a cross.

North of Quainton is Claydon House, also open to the public. It belongs to the National Trust (0296-730349/730693). If you want to visit and look closely, choose a bright day because some of the rooms still don't have electricity.

Claydon House was the home of Sir Edmund Verney, a curious man torn by conflicting loyalties. In the Civil War he was a convinced anti-monarchist. On the other hand he was a friend of the king.

"I have eaten his bread, served him for near thirty years and will not do so base a thing as forsake him, but choose rather to lose my life (which I am sure I shall do)," he said. The king was impressed and promoted him. Oliver Cromwell was less pleased and executed him.

It was all part of a run of bad luck. He was the king's standard bearer at the Battle of Edgehill. "He who takes this banner from my hand must first hew my hand from my body!"

Sadly for him, somebody did.

Quainton to Berkhamsted: 35 Miles

Go straight through pretty crocus-lined lanes and out of Quainton. Turn **left** at a **T-junction** 1 mile later, then **left** again 1 mile afterward, immediately *before* an overhead railroad bridge ("Grendon Underwood, Brill, Bicester") and follow to and across the A41 road ("Wotton Underwood").

Turn **left** on the **A41** instead and you'll find **Waddesdon Manor.** Outside it looks unremarkable. Inside it's spectacular. The Rothschilds commissioned a French architect to make it look as much like a chateau as he could. He did it with great enthusiasm and success and it's the only place outside France that you'll see anything like it. Again, it's held for the people by the National Trust (0296-651211).

The **lane** after the A41 is pleasant, eventually skirting the woods and lakes of Wotton House. Turn **left** at the **T-junction** ("Wotton, Dorton, Thame"). Now follow signs to **Ashendon** (42 miles) and **Cuddington** (45 miles). Continue through the village, past The Crown, on the **Aylesbury road,** to meet the **A418** from Aylesbury to **Thame** (pronounced *Tame*).

Thame has a broad main street packed like a medieval fair during Thame Week; it's a charming town, with buildings of every style, and a good place for a food-and-coffee diversion.

To your left at the **junction** is a ruined folly, overgrandly called Dinton Castle. An old aristo called Sir John Vanhattem used it to house his fossil collection in the 18th century, and ammonites are still stuck in the walls.

Cross the A418 ("Dinton, Ford"), and go into **Dinton.** The Hall here was owned, along with many other people over the centuries, by one Simon Mayne. It was he who signed Charles I's death warrant at the end of the Civil War. This pleased Oliver Cromwell enormously and Cromwell's sword is still in the house.

Things then went downhill for Simon. He ended his days in the Tower of London, which upset his servant John Bigg so much that he spent the rest of his life as a recluse, begging and foraging for food. Bigg's story is remembered in the sign of a pub in **Ford** called The Dinton Hermit.

From Dinton, go **left** at the **crossroads** just before Ford village. Go **right** at the next **crossroads** (50 miles) through Bishopstone to a **railroad crossing** (52 miles). Cross the tracks and then turn immediately **right** into **Terrick**. Dead ahead, up on the hill, you'll see a monument. It remembers the men of Buckinghamshire who died in the Boer War in South Africa and marks the highest point of the

The clean, grassy lines and lonely stone stumps of Berkhamsted Castle mark the start of the Chilterns and The Vale of Aylesbury ride. (English Heritage)

Chiltern hills, the summit of Coombe Hill at 850 feet. Word has it that you can see St. Paul's Cathedral on a good day.

In Terrick, turn **left** past the Terrick sign, then immediately **right** ("Butlers Cross, Ellesborough") into **Chalkshire Road**. Go to the **junction** at **Butlers Cross** (54 miles) and turn **left** into **WEN-DOVER** (55 miles) on the **B4010.**

If you want another excursion, you could go straight on at Butlers Cross; after 1 mile it'll bring you to Chequers, the country house of the prime minister of the day. It was given to the nation to mark the end of the first world war. It's not open to the public.

As you go toward Wendover, you're skirting the Chilterns, and you'll start riding against the grain of the land. Pass the station in Wendover, ignore the A413 and go down through the town to a **roundabout.** Take the **A4011 exit** marked Tring and RAF Halton, but then turn immediately **right** ("The Hale") into **Hale Road.**

Now follow signs to **The Hale** and **St. Leonards.** Take care on this lane because it's narrow with high banks. Follow signs to St. Leonards (59 miles), **Buckland Common** and **Cholesbury** (60 miles).

Turn **left** at the common ("Wigginton, Tring") and you come out at a **T-junction** at the back entrance to Champneys (62 miles), a health farm favored by celebrities. Turn **right** ("Chesham, Amersham"), then **left** 1 mile later ("Northchurch"). Turn **right** at the bottom and follow into the outskirts of **BERKHAMSTED**. Turn **left** where you meet the **A416** and it takes you down to Berkhamsted station, where you started (67 miles).

APPENDIX

ADDRESSES
PART I: INTRODUCTION

Accommodation
Youth Hostels Association
   (England and Wales)
Trevelyan House,
   8 St. Stephens Hill
St. Albans AL1 2DY
phone: 0727-55215

Youth Hostels Association
   (Northern Ireland)
93 Dublin Road
Belfast BT2 7HF
phone: 0232-24733

Youth Hostels Association
   (Scotland)
7 Glebe Crescent
Stirling FK8 2JA
phone: 0786-51181

Bicycling
British Cycling Federation
36 Rockingham Road
Kettering NN16 8HG
phone: 0536-412211

Cyclists Touring Club
69 Meadrow
Godalming, Surrey GU7 3HS
phone: 0483-417217

Tandem Club
25 Hendred Way
Abingdon OX14 2AN

Maps and Roads
Byways and Bridleways Trust
The Granary
Charlcutt, Calne SN11 9HL

The Countryside Commission
   (rights of way)
19-23 Albert Road
Manchester M19 2EQ
phone: 061-224 6287

Forestry Commission (rights of
   way on its land)
231 Corstorphine Road
Edinburgh EH12 7AT
phone: 031-334 0303

Forestry Commission (rights of
   way in North York Moors
   National Park)
42 Eastgate
Pickering, Yorks YO18 7DP

Ordnance Survey (maps)
Romsey Road
Southampton SO9 4DH

Tourism
Association of Railway Preser-
   vation Societies
6 Ullswater Grove
Alresford, Hampshire
   SO24 9NP

British Tourist Authority
64 Thames Tower, Blacks Road
London W6 1EL
phone: 071-730 0791

British Tourist Authority
40 W. 57th Street
New York, NY 10019
(212) 581-4700

British Tourist Authority
94 Cumberland Street, Suite 600
Toronto, ON M5R 3N3 Canada
(416) 925-6326

British Tourist Authority
625 N. Michigan Avenue, Suite 150
Chicago, IL 60611
(312) 787-0490

British Tourist Authority
The World Travel Center
350 S. Figueroa Street, Suite 450
Los Angeles, CA 90071
(213) 628-3525

British Rail Travel Centre
12 Regent Street
London SW1Y 4PD
phone: 071-730 3400; 071-928
    2113 Gatwick Express

BritRail Travel International
630 Third Avenue
New York, NY 10017
(212) 559-5400

BritRail Travel International
94 Cumberland Street, Suite 601
Toronto, ON M5R 1A3 Canada
(416) 929-3333

BritRail Travel International
409 Granville Street
Vancouver, BC V6C 1T2 Canada
(604) 683-6896

English Heritage
PO Box 1BB
London W1A 1BB
phone: 071-973 3457

English Tourist Board
4 Grosvenor Gardens
London SW1W 0DU
phone: 071-730 3400

London subway services
phone: 071-222 1234 (24 hours)

National Trust
42 Queen Anne's Gate
London SW1H 9AS
phone: 081-464 1111

National Trust for Scotland
Charlotte Square
Edinburgh EH2 4DU

Scottish Tourist Board
19 Cockspur Street
London SW1 5BL
phone: 071-930 8661

Scottish Tourist Board
23 Ravelston Terrace
Edinburgh EH4 3EU
phone: 031-332 2433

Wales Tourist Board
2 Fitzalan Road
Cardiff CF2 1UY
phone: 0222-27281

PART II: YOUR ROAD TO BRITAIN

The Garden of England

Attractions

Alfriston Clergy House
phone: 0323-870001

Bluebell Railway
phone: 082572-2370

Brighton Royal Pavilion
phone: 0273-603005

Canterbury Cathedral
phone: 0227-762862

Chartwell (Churchill's home)
phone: 0732-866368

Emmetts Garden
phone: 073275-367

Ightam Mote
phone: 0732-810378

Knole Park (Sevenoaks)
phone: 0732-450608

Leeds Castle
phone: 0622-765400

Quebec House (Westerham)
phone: 0959-62206)

Romney, Hythe and
Dymchurch railroad
phone: 0679-62353

Sandgate castle
phone: 0303-221881

Sheffield Park
phone: 0825-790655

Information

Kent County Council
(cycling info)
Springfield
Maidstone ME14 2LL
phone: 0622-696165

Sealink (ferry operator to
Dieppe)
phone: 0273-514131

West Sussex County Council
(cycling info)
Tower Street
Chichester PO19 1RL
phone: Chichester 777420

Tourist Offices

The Gatehouse, Old Palace
Gardens, Mill Street
Maidstone ME15 6YE
phone: 0622-602169

34 St. Margarets Street
Canterbury CT1 2TG
phone: 0227-766567

Harbour Street
Folkestone CT20 1QN
phone: 0303-58594

Prospect Road Car Park
Hythe CT21 5NH
phone: 0303-267799

4 Roberston Terrace
Hastings TN34 1EZ
phone: 0424-718888

The Fishmarket, The Stade
Hastings TN34 1EZ
phone: 0424-718888

Castle Car Park
Pevensey BN24 5LE
phone: 0323-761444

Cornfield Road
Eastbourne BN21 4QL
phone: 0323-411600

Seafront
Eastbourne
phone: 0323-411800

Station Approach
Seaford BN25 2AR
phone: 0323-897426

88 High Street
Battle TN33 0AQ
phone: 04246 3721

54 Old Steine
Brighton BN1 1EQ
phone: 0273-23755

Lewes House, 32 High Street
Lewes BN7 2LX
phone: 0273-483448

Buckhurst Lane
Sevenoaks TN13 1LQ
phone: 0732-450305

The Isle of Wight
Attractions
Bembridge windmill
phone: 0983-873945

Havenstreet steam railroad
phone: 0983-882204

Information
Hovercraft info
phone: 0983-65241

Red Funnel Line
   (Southampton ferry)
phone: 0703-330333

Sealink (ferries)
phone: 0705-827744

Tourist Office
The Car Park, Church Litten
Newport, Isle of Wight
   PO30 1JU
phone: 0983-525450

The New Forest
Attractions
National Motor Museum
phone: 0590-612345

Information
Southampton ferry
phone: 0703-843203 or
   0703-333584

Tourist Offices
Above Bar
Southampton SO9 4XF
phone: 0703-221106

John Montagu Building
Beaulieu SO42 7ZN
phone: 0590-612345

Poole and The Purbecks
Attractions
Brownsea Island
phone: 0202-707744

Corfe Castle
phone: 0929-480921

Tourist Offices
The Quay
Poole BH15 1HE
phone: 0202-673322

Westover Road
Bournemouth BH21 2BU
phone: 0202-789789

The White Horse, Shore Road
Swanage BH19 1LB
phone: 0929-422885

***Salisbury, The Plain
and Stonehenge***
Tourist Offices
Fish Row
Salisbury SP1 1EJ
phone: 0722-334956

***A Journey Round
Cider Country***
Attractions
American Museum
phone: 0225-460503

Information
County of Avon Council (Bath-
to-Bristol cycle-path guide)
PO Box 41
Avon House North, St. James
Barton
Bristol BS99 7SG

Tourist Offices
Abbey Church Yard
The Collonades, 11-13 Bath
Street
Bath BA1 1SW
phone: 0225-462831

1 Narrow Quay
Bristol BS1 4QA
phone: 0272-260767

The Gorge
Cheddar BS27 3QE
phone: 0934-744071

1 Marchant's Buildings,
Northload Street
Glastonbury BA6 9JJ
phone: 0458-32954

Town Hall, Market Place
Wells BA5 2RB
phone: 0749-72552

The Forest of Dean
Tourist Office
Dean Forest railway
phone: 0594-843423 days;
0452-84625 eves.

The Gatehouse, High Street
Chepstow NP6 5LH
phone: 02912-3772

A Trip over Long Mynd
Tourist Offices
Church Street
Church Stretton SY6 6DQ
phone: 0694-723133

Castle Street
Ludlow, Shrops S48 1AS
phone: 0584-875053

Chester and Shrewsbury
Tourist Offices
Chester Visitors Centre
Vicars Lane
Chester CH1 1QX
phone: 0244-351609

Chester Tourist Information
Town Hall, Northgate Street
Chester CH1 2HJ
phone: 0244-313126

The Square
Shrewsbury SY1 1LH
phone: 0743-50761

Wensleydale
Tourist Offices
National Park Centre, Station
Yard
Hawes DL8 3NT
phone: 0969-667450

Town Hall, Highgate
Kendal LA9 4DL
phone: 0539-725758

Aches in The Lakes
Information
Lake District weather service
phone: 09662-5151

Tourist Office
Ravenglass and Eskdale
Railway Station
Ravenglass, Cumbria
CA18 1SW
phone: 0229-717278

*Dumfries and
The Solway Firth*
Attractions
Burns House
phone: 0387-55297

Tourist Offices
Dumfries and Galloway Tourist
Board
Douglas House
Newton Stewart DG8 6DQ
phone: 0671-2549

Scottish Tourist Board
19 Cockspur Street
London SW1 5BL
phone: 071-9308661

Whitesands
Dumfries, Dumfries and
Galloway
phone: 0387-53862

Car Park
Dalbeattie, Dumfries and
Galloway
phone: 0556-610117

The Magic of Lindisfarne
Attractions
Alnwick Castle
phone: 0665-510777

Bamburgh Castle
phone: 06684-208

Chillingham Castle
phone: 06685-390 or 06685-359

Chillingham Wild Cattle
Association
phone: 06685-213

Farne Islands (bird-watching)
phone: 0665-721099

Howick Hall Gardens
phone: 0665-577285

Lindisfarne Castle
phone: 0289-89244

Lindisfarne Priory
phone: 0289-89200

Tourist Offices
Castlegate Car Park
Berwick TD15 1JS
phone: 0289-330733

The Shambles
Alnwick NE66 1TN
phone: 0665-510665

Car Park, Seafield Road
Seahouses NE68 7SR
phone: 0665-720884

Bus station car park, High
  Street
Wooler NE71 8LD
phone: 0668-81602

The Manor House (information
  on Hadrian's Wall)
Hallgate
Hexham NE46 1XD
phone: 0434-605225

The Gentle Vale of York
Attractions
York cyclists' rally (June)
phone: 0483-417217

Tourist Offices
De Grey Rooms, Exhibition
  Square
York YO1 2HB
phone: 0904-621756

York railroad station, Station
  Road
York YO2 2AY
phone: 0904-643700

Lincoln and The Wolds
Attractions
Tattershall Castle
phone: 0526-42543

Tourist Offices
9 Castle Hill
Lincoln LN1 3AA
phone: 0522-529828

21 The Cornhill
Lincoln LN5 7HB
phone: 0522-812971

Beautiful Norfolk
Attractions
Aylsham-to-Wroxham railroad
phone: 0263-733858

Bircham Windmill
phone: 048523-393

Blicking Hall
phone: 0263-733084

Cockthorpe Hall Toy Museum
phone: 0328-830293

Fakenham Gasworks Museum
phone: 0328-851696

Holkham Hall
phone: 0328-710227

Houghton Hall
phone: East Rudham 569

Langham glass blowers
phone: 0328-830511

Mannington Hall
phone: 026387-4175

Norwich boat rides to the Broads
phone: 0603-501220

Oxburgh Hall
phone: 036621-258

Walsingham guided tours
phone: 0328-820250

Walsingham music festival
  (August)
phone: 0328-820399

Wolferton museum (royal and
  railroad artifacts)
phone: 0485-540674

Wymondham railroad station
(privately owned)
phone: 0953-606433

Information
John Bean (Blakeney sailor for
seal-watching excursions)
phone: 0263-740038

Jim Temple (Blakeney sailor
for seal-watching excursions)
phone: 0263-740791

Tourist Offices
Guildhall, Goal Street
Norfolk NR2 1NF
phone: 0603-666071

Shire Hall Museum
Walsingham, Norfolk
NR22 6BP
phone: 0328-820510

Red Lion House, Market Place
Fakenham, Norfolk NR21 9BY
phone: 0328-851981

The Old Gaol House, Saturday
Market Place
King's Lynn PE30 5AS
phone: 0553-763044

The Glory of Middle England
Attractions
Blenheim Palace
phone: 0993-811325

Cornbury deer park
phone: 0789-470277

Ragley Hall
phone: 0789-762090

Royal Shakespeare theatre
phone: 0789-296655 (backstage
tours) or 0789-295623 (box
office)

Shakespeare Birthplace Trust
phone: 0789-204016

Warwick Castle
phone: 0926-495421

Tourist Offices
Jephson Lodge, The Parade
Leamington Spa,
Warks CV32 4AB
phone: 0926-311470

Centre of Tourism
Civic Hall, Market Place, 14
Rother Street
Stratford-upon-Avon
phone: 0789-294466

Hensington Road
Woodstock OX7 1JQ
phone: 0993-811038

St. Aldate's
Oxford OX1 1DY
phone: 0865-726871

Town Hall, Market Square
Witney OX8 6AG
phone: 0993-775802

Sheep Street
Burford OX8 4LP
phone: 099382-3558

1 Cotswold Court
Broadway WR12 7AA
phone: 0386-852937

The Almonry Museum,
    Abbey Gate
Evesham WR11 4BG
phone: 0386-446944

Chilterns and The Vale of Aylesbury
Attractions
Claydon House (Quainton)
phone: 0296-730349 or
    0296-730693

Waddesdon Manor
phone: 0296-651211

Tourist Offices
(not open year-round)
Berkhamsted Library, Kings
    Road
Berkhamsted HP4 3DB
phone: 04427-864545

County Hall, Walton Street
Aylesbury HP20 1UA
phone: 0296-395000

Clock Tower, High Street
Wendover HP22 6OU
phone: 0296-623056

INDEX

ABOUT THE AUTHOR

Why take advice from a man who once slept in a churchyard in a snowstorm because he hadn't the energy to cycle further or the money for a hotel? Answer: because anyone who's done that (and more) can pass on valued tips, all learned the hard way. Les Woodland has been riding bikes for thirty years and knows Britain inside out. He lives with five bicycles, much clutter and one wife in a picture-book stone cottage in central eastern England. Author of nine books on cycle touring and a BBC radio broadcaster, he has edited and contributed to many other cycling publications in Britain and elsewhere.